Excel
Basic Skills

Year 1
Ages 6–7

English

Donna Gibbs

PASCAL PRESS

Contents

Introduction

The aim of the ***Excel*** **Basic Skills English** series is to build on and reinforce students' basic skills in English. Each book in the series supports the requirements of Australian Curriculum English at each year level.

The ***Excel*** **Basic Skills English** series consists of seven books, one for each year level, from Kindergarten/Foundation to Year 6. The series is supported by other books in the ***Excel*** **Basic Skills** and **Advanced Skills** series.

Structure of the book

This book contains:

- thirty carefully graded double-page units of teaching and learning activities.
  - **Unit A** includes a sample informative, imaginative or persuasive text on subject matter relevant to a range of curriculum areas, and deals with **Reading and Comprehension skills**.
  - **Unit B** deals with the language conventions of **Spelling**, **Vocabulary**, **Grammar** and **Punctuation**.
- four double-page **revision units**.
- four double-page **NAPLAN-style Tests**.

How to use this book

- Students should complete one unit per week. A suggested plan would be to complete the Unit A page for the week on one day and the Unit B page on another day of the same week.
- At the end of a sequence of units students should undertake the applicable Revision units. If students find particular revision questions difficult they should revisit those areas in the previous sequence of units.
- After appropriate revision activities students should undertake the NAPLAN-style Test for those units. The revision work and testing should be completed on different days.

How to use this book with the *Excel* Basic Skills Mathematics series

For a complete **weekly English and Mathematics program** use this book in conjunction with the ***Excel*** *Basic Skills Mathematics Year 1* book. This way a student will have work set for four days a week—two days for English and two days for Mathematics.

How to assess students' progress

- A template is included in each book of the series that outlines the knowledge and skills targeted by the questions in that book. (Please see page 6.)
- The questions move through the subtopics of English in exactly the same order in each book but as there are more questions and more complex material included in later years of the Kindergarten/Foundation to Year 6 continuum, the question numbers vary across the books.
- The results of the work undertaken in each unit can be recorded on the marking grids. Please see the example on page 4. The marking grids on pages 6 and 7 are easy-to-use diagnostic tools that indicate where students' strengths and weaknesses lie in relation to specific areas of English. These results can be used to gather extra information about students' progress and their further revision needs.

The *Excel* Basic Skills and Advanced Skills series

If students are experiencing difficulty, require additional practice or need extension in any area of the course, further books are available to support them in the ***Excel*** **Basic Skills** and **Advanced Skills** series. (Please see the comprehensive list of ***Excel*** books on page 5.)

The *Excel* step-by-step improvement plan

Step 1

Read the introduction on page 3.

Step 2

Read the text below, along with the further explanation about the question templates and marking grids on pages 6–7.

- **Question templates**
  These outline the knowledge and skills targeted by the questions in the book.
  Remember that the questions move through the subtopics of English in exactly the same order in each unit of the book.
- **Marking grids**
  The results of the work undertaken in each unit can be recorded on the marking grids.
  These are an easy-to-use diagnostic tool that indicate where each student's strengths and weaknesses are in relation to specific areas of English.
  These results can be used to gather extra information about each student's progress and their further revision needs. For example, see the sample marking grid in the right-hand column:
  - If a student is consistently getting more than one in five questions wrong in any topic they need help in this area.
  - When marking answers on the grid, simply mark incorrect answers with 'X' in the appropriate box. This will result in a graphical representation of areas needing further work. An example has been done above for the first five units. If a question has several parts, it should be counted as wrong if one or more mistakes are made.
  - Remember that you can identify exactly what type of questions a student is having difficulty with in a topic. For example, in the grid above the student is having difficulty with Reading and Comprehension inferring questions.

	Literal	Literal	Literal	Literal	Inferring	Inferring
Question	**1**	**2**	**3**	**4**	**5**	**6**
Unit 1					X	
Unit 2						X
Unit 3						
Unit 4						X
Unit 5					X	X
Unit 6						
Unit 7						
Unit 8						
Unit 9						

This grid indicates that the student needs extra help and practice in inferring questions.

Step 3

Refer to page 5: ***Excel* books to help you *get the results you want*!**

- Under each topic there is a comprehensive list of books in our range to help students.
  For example, if a student wants help with Reading and Comprehension inferring questions or is ready to move on to more challenging work the books shown at the top of the next page will help them.
  Each ***Excel*** book has a comprehensive contents page that will help you find the appropriate pages in the book to target the specific topic you want in each subject area.

Excel books to help you *get the results you want!*

Reading and Comprehension

Excel Basic Skills
9781741251654

Excel Basic Skills
9781864413403

Excel Advanced Skills
9781741255683

Spelling

Excel Basic Skills
9781864413410

Excel Advanced Skills
9781741254648

Excel Guides
9781864410617

Vocabulary

Excel Basic Skills
9781864413410

Excel Basic Skills
9781741251623

Excel Advanced Skills
9781741254648

Grammar

Excel Basic Skills
9781864413410

Excel Advanced Skills
9781741254419

Punctuation

Excel Basic Skills
9781864413410

Excel Advanced Skills
9781741254419

Writing

Excel Advanced Skills
9781741254853

General

Excel Basic Skills Core
9781864413366

Reading and Comprehension

QUESTION TEMPLATES

1–4 **Literal**
Answers to these questions are found directly in the text.

5–6 **Inferring**
Answers to these questions need to be worked out from clues in the text.

Spelling

1–2 **Unscramble the letters**
In these questions students unscramble the letters and put them in the correct order to correctly spell words from the text.

3 **Rhyme, word families and alliteration**
In this question, in order to make rhyming words, students need to add a letter to the base form of a word so that its meaning is changed, e.g. *cat*, *rat* and *sat*; to find words that alliterate, students need to look for words in the text that begin with the same sound, e.g. *big*, *bag* and *brown*.

Vocabulary

4–7 **Definitions, synonyms, antonyms and meanings in context**
To answer these questions students need to work out the meanings of words in the context of the text. They need to recognise similarities (synonyms) and differences (antonyms) in meanings.

Grammar

8 **Nouns/Noun groups**
This question deals with aspects of a noun group, e.g. nouns, adjectives and articles.

9 **Verbs/Verb groups**
This question deals with aspects of a verb group.

10 **Adverbials**
This question deals with prepositional phrases and adverbs.

Punctuation

11–12 **Sentences (capital letters, full stops, question marks and exclamation marks)**
These questions deal with ways of punctuating sentences, e.g. adding capital letters, full stops, question marks and exclamation marks.

Reading and Comprehension

MARKING GRID

	Literal	Literal	Literal	Literal	Inferring	Inferring
Question	**1**	**2**	**3**	**4**	**5**	**6**
Unit 1						
Unit 2						
Unit 3						
Unit 4						
Unit 5						
Unit 6						
Unit 7						
Unit 8						
Unit 9						
Unit 10						
Unit 11						
Unit 12						
Unit 13						
Unit 14						
Unit 15						
Unit 16						
Unit 17						
Unit 18						
Unit 19						
Unit 20						
Unit 21						
Unit 22						
Unit 23						
Unit 24						
Unit 25						
Unit 26						
Unit 27						
Unit 28						
Unit 29						
Unit 30						
Question	**1**	**2**	**3**	**4**	**5**	**6**

MARKING GRID

Conventions of Language

	Spelling			Vocabulary				Grammar			Punctuation	
	Unscramble the letters	Unscramble the letters	Rhyme/ Word families/ Alliteration	Definitions	Synonyms	Antonyms	Meaning in context/Word usage	Nouns/ Noun groups	Verbs/ Verb groups	Adverbials	Sentences	Sentences
Question	**1**	**2**	**3**	**4**	**5**	**6**	**7**	**8**	**9**	**10**	**11**	**12**
Unit 1												
Unit 2												
Unit 3												
Unit 4												
Unit 5												
Unit 6												
Unit 7												
Unit 8												
Unit 9												
Unit 10												
Unit 11												
Unit 12												
Unit 13												
Unit 14												
Unit 15												
Unit 16												
Unit 17												
Unit 18												
Unit 19												
Unit 20												
Unit 21												
Unit 22												
Unit 23												
Unit 24												
Unit 25												
Unit 26												
Unit 27												
Unit 28												
Unit 29												
Unit 30												
Question	**1**	**2**	**3**	**4**	**5**	**6**	**7**	**8**	**9**	**10**	**11**	**12**

Reading and Comprehension

The chase

The mouse saw some cheese. The cat saw the mouse. The dog saw the cat. The cat quickly chased the mouse. The dog chased the cat. The mouse escaped to his house. The cat escaped up the tree. The dog went back to his bed.

1. What does the mouse see?
   - **A** the cat
   - **B** some cheese
   - **C** the dog

2. What does the cat chase?
   - **A** the mouse
   - **B** some cheese
   - **C** the dog

3. What does the dog chase?
   - **A** the mouse
   - **B** some cheese
   - **C** the cat

4. Where does the mouse escape to?
   - **A** a tree
   - **B** his house
   - **C** a dog bed

5. Why did the cat go up the tree?
   - **A** The dog was good at climbing trees.
   - **B** The mouse was good at climbing trees.
   - **C** The dog was not good at climbing trees.

6. Why did the dog go back to bed?
   - **A** The cat had escaped from the dog.
   - **B** The dog was sleepy.
   - **C** The mouse had run away.

UNIT 1B

Spelling

1 Unscramble the letters to make words.

A dbe ____________

B hsi ____________

C reet ____________

2 Unscramble the letters to make words.

A seuom ____________

B useoh ____________

C seeche ____________

3 Write words that rhyme with **bed**.

A f__ __ **B** r__ __ **C** w__ __

Vocabulary

4 Which word from the text means **ran after**?

____

5 Circle the word that has a similar meaning to **house**.

tree home bed

6 Cross out the word that does **not** belong.

quickly slowly fast

7 Add a word from the text to the sentence.

The cat ran up the ____________.

Grammar

8 Draw lines from the nouns to label the picture:

cat

dog

mouse

9 Choose a verb from the box to complete the sentence.

go	walk	ran

The mouse ____________ away from the cat.

10 Write a prepositional phrase from the text to tell **where**.

The cat climbed

____________.

Punctuation

Write each sentence correctly beginning with a capital letter and ending with a full stop.

11 The cat chased the mouse

____

____

12 the dog chased the cat

____

____

Reading and Comprehension

Cat facts

Cats:

- sleep a lot
- lick their fur to keep it clean
- see well in the dark
- have four paws with soft pads and claws
- like to hunt small animals, and
- make good pets.

1. How much do cats sleep?
   - **A** a little
   - **B** a lot
   - **C** never
2. How do cats clean their fur?
   - **A** They lick their fur.
   - **B** They roll in puddles.
   - **C** They take a shower.
3. How many paws do cats have?
   - **A** two
   - **B** four
   - **C** six
4. What do cats hunt?
   - **A** middle-sized animals
   - **B** big animals
   - **C** small animals
5. Why do cats make good pets?
   - **A** They can see in the dark.
   - **B** They have claws.
   - **C** They are clean animals.
6. How do cats use their soft paws?
   - **A** to sharpen their claws
   - **B** to move quietly when hunting
   - **C** to clean their fur

Spelling

1 Unscramble the letters to make words.

A ees ____________

B tacs ____________

C urf ____________

2 Unscramble the letters to make words.

A yad ____________

B doog ____________

C wlcas ____________

3 Write words that rhyme with **cats**.

A b ____ B h ____ C m ____

Vocabulary

4 Which word from the text means **without light**?

____

5 Circle the word that has a similar meaning to **hunt**.

lick chase pat

6 Cross out the word that does **not** belong.

see watch sleep

7 Add a word from the text to complete the sentence.

Cats lick their ____________ to keep it clean.

Grammar

8 Draw lines from the nouns to label the picture:

paws fur claws

9 Choose a verb from the box to complete the sentence.

hunts	sleep	chases

Cats ____________ a lot of the time.

10 Write a prepositional phrase from the text to tell **where**.

Cats are good at seeing

____________.

Punctuation

Write each sentence correctly beginning with a capital letter and ending with a full stop.

11 cats have sharp claws

____

12 cats make good pets

____

Reading and Comprehension

Nearly six

In one week Tom will be six years old. He ticks off the days on his calendar. There are still seven more days to wait.

On 4 March it is his birthday and he is having a party in his garden. He will have a birthday cake with candles. Everyone in his class is coming.

1. How long is it until Tom's birthday?
   - **A** one day
   - **B** one week
   - **C** one month

2. What date is his birthday?
   - **A** 4 June
   - **B** 4 May
   - **C** 4 March

3. What sort of cake will he have?
   - **A** birthday
   - **B** apple
   - **C** fruit

4. What will Tom do on his birthday?
   - **A** go to the beach
   - **B** have a party
   - **C** draw on his calendar

5. Who has Tom invited to his party?
   - **A** all of his class
   - **B** some of his class
   - **C** none of his class

6. Why does Tom mark the days off on his calendar?
   - **A** He likes making ticks.
   - **B** He likes seeing his birthday getting closer.
   - **C** He likes calendars.

Spelling

1 Unscramble the letters to make words.

A neo ....

B xis ....

C ffo ....

2 Unscramble the letters to make words.

A vense ....

B sslac ....

C rmoe ....

3 Write words that rhyme with **cake**.

A b ... ... B l ... ... C m ... ...

Vocabulary

4 Which word from the text means **almost**?

....

5 Circle the word that has a similar meaning to **garden**.

backyard farm field

6 Cross out the word that does **not** belong.

more less extra

7 Add a word from the text to the sentence.

Tom will blow out the .... at his party.

Grammar

8 Draw lines from the nouns to label the picture:

cake candles calendar

9 Choose a verb from the box to complete the sentence.

waits	ticks	sees

Tom .... off each date on his calendar.

10 Write a prepositional phrase from the text to tell **where**.

Tom is having his party

....

Punctuation

Write each sentence correctly beginning with a capital letter and ending with a full stop.

11 Tom will soon be six

....

....

12 the party is on 4 March

....

....

Reading and Comprehension

Letter to my uncle

Dear Uncle Jack

I fell over at school today. I cut my knee badly on a hard stone. My friend found the teacher. The teacher was kind to me. She put a bandage on my knee. I nearly cried but I stopped myself. Then she patted my head and said 'What a brave girl.'

Love
Dasha

1. What did Dasha hurt?
   - **A** her arm
   - **B** her hand
   - **C** her knee

2. What cut Dasha's knee?
   - **A** a stone
   - **B** a knife
   - **C** glass

3. Who found the teacher?
   - **A** Dasha
   - **B** Dasha's friend
   - **C** Uncle Jack

4. What did the teacher put on Dasha's knee?
   - **A** a bandage
   - **B** glue
   - **C** water

5. 'I fell over at school today.' Who is "I"?
   - **A** the teacher
   - **B** Dasha
   - **C** Dasha's friend

6. Why does Dasha's teacher say Dasha is brave?
   - **A** She sees her crying.
   - **B** She sees her knee is cut.
   - **C** She sees her trying not to cry.

Spelling

1 Unscramble the letters to make words.

A tuc ____________

B rea ____________

C hdea ____________

2 Unscramble the letters to make words.

A rgil ____________

B rhad ____________

C nkee ____________

3 Write words that rhyme with **cut**.

A ____ B ____ C ____

Vocabulary

4 Which word from the text means **slit**?

____

5 Circle the word that has a similar meaning to **hard**.

weak soft firm

6 Cross out the word that does **not** belong.

unkind cruel kind

7 Add a word from the text to the sentence.

I fell and hurt my ____________.

Grammar

8 Draw lines from the nouns to label the picture:

girl

teacher

knee

9 Choose a verb from the box to complete the sentence.

watch	feel	cry

Did you ____________ when you cut your knee?

10 Write a prepositional phrase from the text to tell **where**.

The teacher put a bandage

____________.

Punctuation

Write each sentence correctly beginning with a capital letter and ending with a full stop.

11 I tried not to cry

____

12 i fell over

____

Lunchtime

To make an egg and lettuce roll you need:

- a bread roll
- some butter
- an egg
- lettuce
- a saucepan of water
- a knife.

Then you:

- break open the roll and butter it
- boil the egg in the water for eight minutes
- peel the egg and chop it up
- wash and chop up the lettuce
- put the egg and the lettuce into the roll.

1. How much butter do you need?
   - **A** lots
   - **B** a huge bit
   - **C** some

2. What do you boil?
   - **A** the egg
   - **B** the lettuce
   - **C** the bread

3. What does the water go in?
   - **A** the saucepan
   - **B** the roll
   - **C** the egg

4. What do you do to the lettuce?
   - **A** boil it
   - **B** wash it and chop it up
   - **C** butter it

5. What do you need that isn't on the list?
   - **A** some jam
   - **B** some cheese
   - **C** a stove

6. At which meal would the writer eat an egg and lettuce roll?
   - **A** breakfast
   - **B** lunch
   - **C** dinner

Spelling

1 Unscramble the letters to make words.

A tpu ______

B gge ______

C leep ______

2 Unscramble the letters to make words.

A pcho ______

B libo ______

C fknie ______

3 Write words that rhyme with **chop**.

A ___ B ___ C ___

Vocabulary

4 Which word from the text means **take the shell off**?

______

5 Circle the word that has a similar meaning to **chop**.

stir cut melt

6 Cross out the word that does **not** belong.

break mend cut

7 Add a word from the text to the sentence.

I made an egg and lettuce

______.

Grammar

8 Draw lines from the nouns to label the picture:

egg

roll

lettuce

9 Choose a verb from the box to complete the sentence.

break	touch	shut

You have to ______ the roll open.

10 Write a prepositional phrase from the text to tell **where**.

I put the lettuce and the egg

______.

Punctuation

Write each sentence correctly beginning with a capital letter and ending with a full stop.

11 I boiled the egg

______

12 she made an egg roll

______

______

Reading and Comprehension

Counting

Want to have fun?
Then let's count from
one.
One, two. Buckle my shoe.
Three, four. Knock at the
door.
Five, six. Pick up sticks.
Seven, eight. Lay them
straight.
Nine, ten. Do it again.

1. What do you buckle?
   - **A** the door
   - **B** the sticks
   - **C** your shoe

2. What do you knock at?
   - **A** the door
   - **B** your shoe
   - **C** the sticks

3. What do you pick up?
   - **A** your shoe
   - **B** the door
   - **C** sticks

4. What do you lay straight?
   - **A** the sticks
   - **B** your shoe
   - **C** the door

5. What do you do again?
   - **A** Lay the sticks straight.
   - **B** Knock at the door.
   - **C** Count from one to ten.

6. Why are there five ladybirds in the picture?
   - **A** The others ran away.
   - **B** Six ladybirds would not fit.
   - **C** It shows how many ladybirds make the number five.

Spelling

1 Unscramble the letters to make words.

A eth

B nuf

C nnie

2 Unscramble the letters to make words.

A rood

B ckip

C ourf

3 Write words that rhyme with **pick**.

A ____ B ____ C ____

Vocabulary

4 Which word from the text means **another time**?

5 Circle the word that has a similar meaning to **straight**.

crooked bent neatly

6 Cross out the word that does **not** belong.

knock bang tickle

7 Add a word from the text to complete the sentence.

Would you unbuckle my

____ please?

Grammar

8 Draw lines from the nouns to label the picture:

mice houses hearts

9 Choose a verb from the box to complete the sentence.

jumps	gives	do

I have to ____ it again.

10 Write a prepositional phrase from the text to tell **where**.

I will knock

____.

Punctuation

Write each sentence correctly beginning with a capital letter and ending with a full stop.

11 we said the poem

12 we had fun

Reading and Comprehension

For sale

Our goat, Sam, is for sale. Soon we are moving to a unit in the city. We can't keep a goat in a unit! Sam has soft, white hair and a beard! She likes to eat grass but she eats almost anything. I will miss Sam. Please buy our goat. Call Tom on 9898333.

1. Who is Sam?
   - **A** Tom
   - **B** a girl
   - **C** a goat

2. Where is Tom going to live?
   - **A** in a farm house
   - **B** in a unit
   - **C** in the country

3. What kind of hair does Sam have?
   - **A** hard
   - **B** wiry
   - **C** soft

4. What does Sam like to eat?
   - **A** grass
   - **B** units
   - **C** nothing

5. Why does Tom need to sell his goat?
   - **A** He needs the money.
   - **B** He dislikes the goat.
   - **C** Goats aren't allowed to live in units.

6. Why will Tom miss Sam?
   - **A** He doesn't have any friends.
   - **B** He won't see Sam any more.
   - **C** Sam likes Tom.

Spelling

1 Unscramble the letters to make words.

A uyb ____________

B ssim ____________

C ssgra ____________

2 Unscramble the letters to make words.

A ntiu ____________

B ycti ____________

C ftos ____________

3 Write words that rhyme with **goat**.

A ________ B ________ C ________

Vocabulary

4 Which word from the text means **hair that grows on the chin**?

____

5 Circle the word that has a similar meaning to **soon**.

more always shortly

6 Cross out the word that does **not** belong.

soft stiff hard

7 Add a word from the text to the sentence.

Call Tom if you want to buy

his ____________.

Grammar

8 Draw lines from the nouns to label the picture:

goat

beard

grass

9 Choose a verb from the box to complete the sentence.

cry	help	miss

I will ____________ Sam when she is sold.

10 Write a prepositional phrase from the text to tell **where**.

Our new unit is

____________.

Punctuation

Write each sentence correctly beginning with a capital letter and ending with a full stop.

11 our goat lives on a farm

____

12 goats eat anything

____

Reading and Comprehension

1 Choose a word from the box to go in each space.

have	birthday	one	six	party	days	class

In ________________ week Tom will be ________________ years old. He ticks off the ________________ on his calendar. There are still seven more days to wait. His ________________ is on 4 March.

He is having a ________________ in his garden. He will ________________ a birthday cake with candles. Everyone in his ________________ is coming.

2 Choose a word from the box to go in each space.

my	nearly	friend	hard	head	me	teacher

Dear Uncle Jack

I fell over at school today. I cut my knee badly on a ______________ stone. My ______________ found the teacher. The ______________ was kind to ______________. She put a bandage on ______________ knee. I ______________ cried but I stopped myself. Then she patted my ______________ and said 'What a brave girl.'

Love

Dasha

Spelling

3 Add nouns to label the pictures.

____

______________________ ______________________

Vocabulary

4 Circle the word that means **a bun made from bread.**

I ate an egg roll for lunch.

5 Circle the word that means **animals you keep in your home.**

Cats make good pets.

6 Circle the word that has a similar meaning to **at this time.**

then now soon

7 Cross out the word that does **not** belong.

big huge tiny

Grammar

8 Choose a prepositional phrase from the box to complete the sentences.

on my cake	in the city	in a bed

A We live ______________________.

B I had candles ______________________.

C I sleep ______________________.

Punctuation

9 Write this sentence correctly.

it is good to have a friend

____

Reading

Letter to my nan

Dear Nan,

We are in our new house. We have a small garden. It is in the city. I miss our goat a lot. I cried when I left it. Mum said now I can have a small pet of my own. I like cats. I hope we will get a cat.

Love
Molly

1. Who is Molly writing to?
   - **A** her mum
   - **B** her nan
   - **C** her diary

2. What size garden does Molly have?
   - **A** small
   - **B** big
   - **C** huge

3. What does Molly miss?
   - **A** the city
   - **B** their garden
   - **C** their goat

4. What does Molly's mum say she can have now?
   - **A** a cat
   - **B** a dog
   - **C** a small pet

5. Why was the goat left?
   - **A** It wanted to stay at the old house.
   - **B** It didn't like the new house.
   - **C** A city is not a good place for a goat.

6. Who owned the goat?
   - **A** Nan
   - **B** Molly's family
   - **C** Molly

NAPLAN-STYLE 1 CONVENTIONS OF LANGUAGE TEST

Spelling

1 Which word is spelt correctly?

A gote **B** goat **C** gott

2 Find the spelling mistake and write the word correctly on the line.

The cat is in the howse. ____________________

3 Which word rhymes with **pet**?

A seat **B** set **C** sat

Vocabulary

4 Which word means **at this time**?

A then **B** now **C** soon

5 Which word means the same as the underlined word?

We have a <u>small</u> garden.

A big **B** nice **C** tiny

Grammar

6 Which verb completes the sentence correctly?

Can I ____________ a pet of my own, please?

A had **B** haves **C** have

7 Circle the words that tell **where** in this sentence.

Our new house is in the city.

Punctuation

8 Which sentence is punctuated correctly?

A She has one cat and two dogs

B she has one cat and two dogs.

C She has one cat and two dogs.

Reading and Comprehension

On the bus

Our school bus is yellow with black wheels. We have a driver called Sam.

Sally did not sit next to me today.

'Why were you mean to me, Bill?' she asked.

'I don't know. I'm sorry, Sally,' I replied.

I hope she will sit next to me on the bus in the morning.

1. What colour are the wheels of the bus?

   A black

   B blue

   C yellow

2. What is the bus driver's name?

   A Bill

   B Sally

   C Sam

3. Who does not sit with Bill?

   A the bus driver

   B Sally's friend

   C Sally

4. What kind of bus is it?

   A a toy bus

   B a school bus

   C a double-decker bus

5. Why didn't Sally sit next to Bill?

   A She wanted to sit with her friend.

   B She didn't like Bill.

   C She thought Bill might be mean again.

6. Why does Bill want Sally to sit with him on the bus?

   A He likes Sally.

   B He likes being mean to Sally.

   C He doesn't have any friends.

UNIT 8B

Spelling

1 Unscramble the letters to make words.

A usb ____________

B hse ____________

C sdai ____________

2 Unscramble the letters to make words.

A ooschl ____________

B xent ____________

C phoe ____________

3 Write words that rhyme with **will**.

A ________ B ________ C ________

Vocabulary

4 Which word from the text means **unkind**?

____

5 Circle the word that has a similar meaning to **next to**.

near apart away

6 Cross out the word that does **not** belong.

replied said went

7 Add a word from the text to complete the sentence.

Our bus has four black

____________.

Grammar

8 Draw lines from the nouns to label the picture:

bus

driver

wheels

9 Choose a verb from the box to complete the sentence.

are	was	is

Sally said I ____________ mean to her.

10 Write a prepositional phrase from the text to tell **when**.

Bill hopes Sally will sit next to him

____________.

Punctuation

A sentence begins with a capital letter. If it asks a question it ends with a question mark.
Write each sentence correctly.

11 are you sorry

____

12 do you go to school

____

Reading and Comprehension

A new baby?

Dad got my old pram from the shed. He and Mum painted it. I am far too old for a pram. Mum got a baby's milk bottle and a new bear at the shops last week. I have a bear already. I don't drink milk from a baby's bottle. Who do you think the new things are for?

1. What did Dad get from the shed?
   - **A** a bear
   - **B** a pram
   - **C** a bottle

2. Who painted the pram?
   - **A** Dad
   - **B** Mum
   - **C** Dad and Mum

3. What did Mum buy at the shops?
   - **A** a pram
   - **B** a baby
   - **C** a bear

4. Where did Mum get the baby's bottle from?
   - **A** the shops
   - **B** the shed
   - **C** the cupboard

5. The writer is
   - **A** a baby.
   - **B** a child.
   - **C** an old person.

6. Who are the new things for?
   - **A** a new baby
   - **B** a bear
   - **C** the writer

Spelling

1 Unscramble the letters to make words.

A brea ______

B dehs ______

C wen ______

2 Unscramble the letters to make words.

A lkim ______

B ttbole ______

C marp ______

3 Write words that rhyme with **dad**.

A ______ B ______ C ______

Vocabulary

4 Which word from the text means **by this time**?

______

5 Circle the word that has a similar meaning to **used**.

old new fresh

6 Cross out the word that does **not** belong.

now today later

7 Add a word from the text to the sentence.

Some babies drink milk from a ______.

Grammar

8 Draw lines from the nouns to label the picture:

bear pram bottle

9 Choose a verb from the box to complete the sentence.

eat	drink	gives

I don't ______ milk.

10 Write a prepositional phrase from the text to tell **when**.

Mum went to the shops

______.

Punctuation

A sentence begins with a capital letter. If it asks a question it ends with a question mark.
Write each sentence correctly.

11 will the baby cry

______

12 is the pram new

______

Reading and Comprehension

An apple a day

Did you know apples are good for your bones? They have lots of Vitamin C. Take an apple to school in your lunch box. Eat an apple after dinner. Eating an apple helps keep your teeth clean and healthy. An apple a day keeps the doctor away.

1. Are apples good for your bones?
   - **A** yes
   - **B** no
   - **C** maybe
2. Which vitamin do apples have a lot of?
   - **A** Vitamin A
   - **B** Vitamin B
   - **C** Vitamin C
3. What can you take your apple in to school?
   - **A** your teeth
   - **B** your dinner
   - **C** your lunch box
4. What can keep your teeth healthy?
   - **A** eating an apple
   - **B** taking an apple to school
   - **C** putting an apple in your lunch box
5. When is it best to eat an apple?
   - **A** before school
   - **B** after a meal
   - **C** before breakfast
6. Why would an apple a day keep the doctor away?
   - **A** Doctors dislike apples.
   - **B** Apples help keep you healthy.
   - **C** Doctors like apples.

UNIT 10B

Spelling

1 Unscramble the letters to make words.

A obx ______

B yda ______

C ouy ______

2 Unscramble the letters to make words.

A nboes ______

B eetth ______

C pplea ______

3 Write words that rhyme with **eat**.

A ______ B ______ C ______

Vocabulary

4 Which word from the text means **not dirty**?

______

5 Circle the word that has a similar meaning to **lots of**.

plenty none some

6 Cross out the word that does **not** belong.

good bad excellent

7 Add a word from the text to the sentence.

I found an apple in my lunch

______.

Grammar

8 Draw lines from the nouns to label the picture:

apple

doctor

teeth

9 Choose a verb from the box to complete the sentence.

throw	eat	picks

It is good for your health to

______ an apple.

10 Write a prepositional phrase from the text to tell **when**.

I eat an apple ______.

Punctuation

A sentence begins with a capital letter.
If it asks a question it ends with a question mark.
Write each sentence correctly.

11 Do you eat an apple a day

______

______

12 are apples good for you

______

______

UNIT 11A

Reading and Comprehension

Stuck!

Dad and I are at the park this morning. Sam, our dog, is with us. I have my blue ball. We play happily with the ball on the grass. Then Dad kicks the ball very high. I look up into the trees. I see my ball is stuck on a branch. Oh no! Is our game over now?

1. What is Sam?
   - **A** a boy
   - **B** a father
   - **C** a dog

2. What colour is the boy's ball?
   - **A** blue
   - **B** green
   - **C** red

3. What do the boy and his dad play with?
   - **A** Sam
   - **B** a branch
   - **C** a ball

4. Who kicks the ball up high?
   - **A** Dad
   - **B** Sam
   - **C** the boy

5. Why does the ball get stuck in the tree?
   - **A** Sam chases it up the tree.
   - **B** Dad kicks the ball too high.
   - **C** The boy throws it into the tree.

6. Why does the boy think their game is over?
   - **A** It is lunchtime.
   - **B** It is time to go home.
   - **C** They can't reach their ball.

Spelling

1 Unscramble the letters to make words.

A yob ....

B nam ....

C rkpa ....

2 Unscramble the letters to make words.

A oolk ....

B rete ....

C allb ....

3 Write words that rhyme with **ball**.

A .... B .... C ....

Vocabulary

4 Which word from the text means **can't move**?

....

5 Circle the word that has a similar meaning to **over**.

ended started left

6 Cross out the word that does **not** belong.

tall high short

7 Add a word from the text to complete the sentence.

We took my blue ball to the

....

Grammar

8 Draw lines from the nouns to label the picture:

ball grass boy

9 Choose a verb from the box to complete the sentence.

look	play	kicks

Dad ....
the ball up high.

10 Write a prepositional phrase from the text to tell **when**.

We played in the park

....

Punctuation

Write each sentence correctly.

11 I was upset when the ball got stuck

....

....

12 will you help get my ball

....

....

Reading and Comprehension

My favourite book

My favourite book is *The Very Hungry Caterpillar*. There are holes in the pages where the caterpillar eats the fruit. I had fun this morning looking through the holes. Then at the end of the story it was like magic. The caterpillar turned into a butterfly!

by
Kim

1. How hungry is the caterpillar?
   - **A** not very hungy
   - **B** very hungry
   - **C** not at all hungry

2. What does the caterpillar eat in the story?
   - **A** fruit
   - **B** leaves
   - **C** holes

3. What does Kim do with the holes?
   - **A** looks through them
   - **B** looks at them
   - **C** looks over them

4. What is the caterpillar when it wakes?
   - **A** a cocoon
   - **B** a butterfly
   - **C** a book

5. Who put the holes in the pages of the book?
   - **A** Kim
   - **B** caterpillars
   - **C** the person who made the book

6. What makes Kim think of magic?
   - **A** the way holes are made in the book
   - **B** the way the caterpillar turns into a butterfly
   - **C** the way the cocoon is made

Spelling

1 Unscramble the letters to make words.

A nuf ____________

B yrev ____________

C koob ____________

2 Unscramble the letters to make words.

A oooccn ____________

B teracillpar ____________

C utterbyfl ____________

3 Write words that rhyme with **book**.

A _ _ _ _ B _ _ _ _ C _ _ _ _

Vocabulary

4 Which word from the text means **empty spaces**?

____

5 Circle the word that has a similar meaning to **very hungry**.

starving full thirsty

6 Cross out the word that does **not** belong.

munches spits eats

7 Add a word from the text to complete the sentence.

What is the title of your favourite ____________?

Grammar

8 Draw lines from the nouns to label the picture:

books

pages

Kim

9 Choose a verb from the box to complete the sentence.

eat	sips	wants

Caterpillars ____________ leaves.

10 Write a prepositional phrase from the text to tell **when**.

Kim had fun ____________.

Punctuation

Write each sentence correctly.

11 is the story about a caterpillar

____

____

12 Kim likes this story

____

____

UNIT 13A

Reading and Comprehension

Ladybirds

A ladybird is a small insect with a very small head. It has six legs and two pairs of wings. The top pair of wings are yellow, red or orange with black spots. Ladybirds eat insects that eat plants. Farmers like having ladybirds in their crops all the time. I wonder why?

1. A ladybird has a very small
   - **A** wing.
   - **B** leg.
   - **C** head.

2. How many legs does a ladybird have?
   - **A** six
   - **B** two
   - **C** four

3. How many pairs of wings does a ladybird have?
   - **A** one
   - **B** two
   - **C** three

4. Ladybirds eat
   - **A** insects.
   - **B** plants.
   - **C** farmers.

5. Ladybirds live
   - **A** in fields and gardens.
   - **B** inside bedrooms and bathrooms.
   - **C** on the moon and the stars.

6. Why do farmers like ladybirds?
   - **A** They like their colours.
   - **B** They eat pests that eat their crops.
   - **C** They like to see them fly away.

Spelling

1 Unscramble the letters to make words.

A der ____________

B cklab ____________

C klie ____________

2 Unscramble the letters to make words.

A adeh ____________

B potss ____________

C gels ____________

3 Write words that rhyme with **black**.

A ________ B ________ C ________

Vocabulary

4 Which word from the text means **small round marks**?

____

5 Circle the word that has a similar meaning to **small**.

tiny round spotted

6 Cross out the word that does **not** belong.

like dislike hate

7 Add a word from the text to complete the sentence.

I saw a caterpillar eating

____________.

Grammar

8 Draw lines from the nouns to label the picture:

legs head spots

9 Choose a verb from the box to complete the sentence.

learn	like	lose

Farmers ____________ ladybirds.

10 Write a prepositional phrase from the text to tell **when**.

Farmers like ladybirds to be in their crops ____________.

Punctuation

Write each sentence correctly.

11 how many legs does it have

____

____

12 do ladybirds eat plants

____

____

Reading and Comprehension

Please take me home

I live in a home for dogs. I want to live in a home with a family. I have floppy ears, soft brown fur and a sad face. My name is Mr Brown. I love to go for walks. Please visit me very soon and then take me home with you. Will you?

1. Where does the dog live now?
   - **A** in a home
   - **B** in a home for dogs
   - **C** in a home with a family

2. What kind of ears does the dog have?
   - **A** big
   - **B** brown
   - **C** floppy

3. What kind of face does the dog have?
   - **A** sad
   - **B** glad
   - **C** happy

4. What does the dog love to do?
   - **A** eat dog biscuits
   - **B** ask people to visit
   - **C** go for walks

5. Why is the dog called Mr Brown?
   - **A** He is an important dog.
   - **B** He is male and has brown fur.
   - **C** He is always writing letters.

6. Why does the dog want to live in a home with a family?
   - **A** He wants a family of his own.
   - **B** He doesn't have any friends in the dog home.
   - **C** He likes going for walks.

UNIT 14B

Spelling

1 Unscramble the letters to make words.

A mhoe ____________

B easr ____________

C vloe ____________

2 Unscramble the letters to make words.

A brwon ____________

B lliw ____________

C isitv ____________

3 Write words that rhyme with **dogs**.

A ________ B ________ C ________

Vocabulary

4 Which word from the text means **unhappy**?

____

5 Circle the word that has a similar meaning to **soft**.

hard smooth sharp

6 Cross out the word that does **not** belong.

before soon next

7 Add a word from the text to complete the sentence.

Most dogs like to go for

____________.

Grammar

8 Draw lines from the nouns to label the picture:

fur

ears

face

9 Choose a verb from the box to complete the sentence.

wants	has	need

Mr Brown ____________ brown fur and floppy ears.

10 Write a prepositional phrase from the text to tell **when**.

I hope you will visit me

____________.

Punctuation

Write each sentence correctly.

11 I took Mr Brown home with me

____

____

12 does Mr Brown have floppy ears

____

____

Reading and Comprehension

Apples

Farmers pick apples from their trees in the autumn. They pack them in boxes. They are sold in markets and shops. There are many different kinds of apple. They all have their own names. Some apples are called Pink Ladies, others Granny Smiths. Do you have a favourite kind?

1. Who picks the apples?
   - **A** shopkeepers
   - **B** Granny Smith
   - **C** farmers

2. What are apples packed in?
   - **A** boxes
   - **B** shops
   - **C** markets

3. How many kinds of apples are there?
   - **A** two kinds
   - **B** one kind
   - **C** many kinds

4. Where are the apples sold?
   - **A** in markets
   - **B** in fields
   - **C** in farms

5. Why are apples picked in autumn?
   - **A** It is cool for picking.
   - **B** That is when apples are ripe.
   - **C** Farmers are too busy in the other seasons.

6. Why do farmers pack apples in boxes?
   - **A** to transport them to market
   - **B** to keep them clean
   - **C** to get them off the ground

UNIT 15B

Spelling

1 Unscramble the letters to make words.

A rgow ____________

B ldos ____________

C oxseb ____________

2 Unscramble the letters to make words.

A henw ____________

B pplea ____________

C ckap ____________

3 Write words that rhyme with **pack**.

A _ _ _ _ B _ _ _ _ C _ _ _ _

Vocabulary

4 Which word from the text means **not like each other**?

____

5 Circle the word that has a similar meaning to **sort**.

pick kind name

6 Cross out the word that does **not** belong.

many lots few

7 Add a word from the text to complete the sentence.

My favourite kind of ____________ is a Granny Smith.

Grammar

8 Draw lines from the nouns to label the picture:

apple

boxes

trees

9 Choose a verb from the box to complete the sentence.

left	dropped	pick

Farmers ____________ the apples when they are ripe.

10 Write a prepositional phrase from the text to tell **when**.

The apples are picked

____________.

Punctuation

Write each sentence correctly.

11 which is your favourite apple

____

____

____

12 do you like Granny Smiths

____

____

Reading and Comprehension

1 Choose a word from the box to go in each space.

wings	insect	why	black	head	plants	legs

A ladybird is a small ____________________ with a very small ____________________. It has six ____________________ and two pairs of ____________________. The top pair of wings are yellow, red or orange with ____________________ spots. Ladybirds eat insects that eat ____________________. Farmers like having ladybirds in their crops all the time. I wonder ____________________?

2 Choose a word from the box to go in each space.

ears	love	you	home	sad	take	live

I ____________________ in a home for dogs. I want to live in a ____________________ with a family. I have floppy ____________________, soft brown fur and a ____________________ face. My name is Mr Brown. I ____________________ to go for walks. Please visit me very soon and then ____________________ me home with you.

Will ____________________?

Answers

Unit 1A page 8

1. B. See lines 2–3.
2. A. See lines 5–6.
3. C. See lines 6–7.
4. B. See lines 7–9.
5. C. See lines 9–11. You can work out the cat went up the tree to get away from the dog. It knew it would be safe because the dog couldn't climb the tree.
6. A. See lines 9–11. You can work out the dog went back to bed because it had given up trying to catch the cat who kept escaping from him.

Unit 1B page 9

1. A. bed B. his C. tree
2. A. mouse B. house C. cheese
3. A. fed B. red C. wed
4. chased
5. home
6. slowly
7. tree
8. 

9. ran
10. up the tree
11. The cat chased the mouse.
12. The dog chased the cat.

Unit 2A page 10

1. B. See line 3.
2. A. See lines 4–5.
3. B. See line 7.
4. C. See lines 9–10.
5. C. See lines 4–5. You can work out a pet that keeps itself clean won't make the house dirty or spread germs to the family.
6. B. See lines 9–10. You can work out soft paws wouldn't make a noise. This means the small animals won't hear the cat coming after them.

Unit 2B page 11

1. A. see B. cats C. fur
2. A. day B. good C. claws
3. A. bats B. hats C. mats
4. dark
5. chase
6. sleep
7. fur
8. 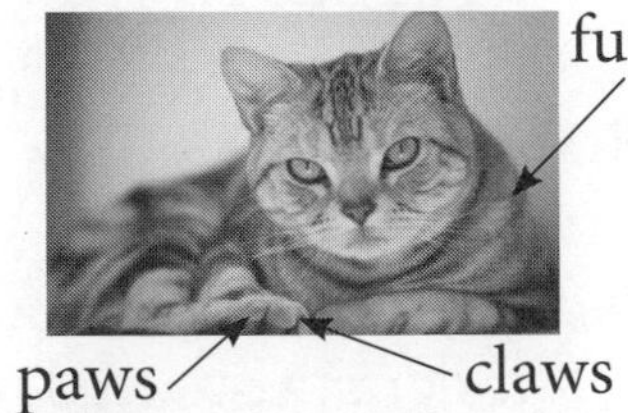

9. sleep
10. in the dark
11. Cats have sharp claws.
12. Cats make good pets.

Unit 3A page 12

1. B. See line 2.
2. C. See line 6.
3. A. See lines 8–9.
4. B. See lines 6–7.
5. A. See lines 10–11. You can work out Tom has invited all of his class since everyone in his class is coming to his party.
6. B. See lines 3–5. You can work out Tom likes to see the number of days left as he marks them off. This shows him his birthday is getting closer.

Unit 3B page 13

1. A. one B. six C. off
2. A. seven B. class C. more
3. A. bake B. lake C. make
4. nearly
5. backyard
6. less
7. candles
8. 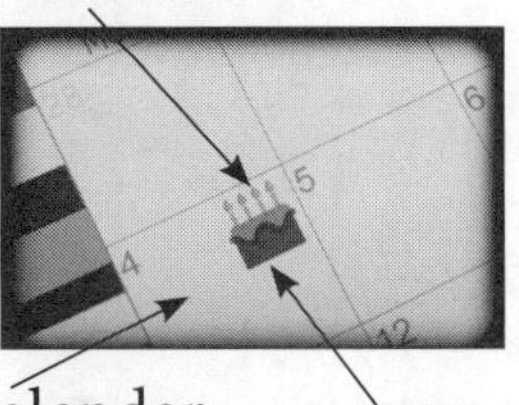

9. ticks
10. in his garden
11. Tom will soon be six.
12. The party is on 4 March.

Unit 4A page 14

1. C. See line 3.
2. A. See lines 3–4.
3. B. See lines 4–5.
4. A. See line 6.
5. B. See line 11. You can work out "I" stands for Dasha as she writes the letter to Uncle Jack.
6. C. See lines 6–7. You can work out the teacher sees that Dasha tries not to cry even

Answers

though she has cut her knee badly. She thinks this is brave of Dasha.

Unit 4B page 15

1. A. cut B. are C. head
2. A. girl B. hard C. knee
3. Answers will vary, e.g. but, gut, hut, jut, nut, rut.
4. cut
5. firm
6. kind
7. knee
8. 

9. cry
10. on my knee
11. I tried not to cry.
12. I fell over.

Unit 5A page 16

1. C. See line 4.
2. A. See line 11.
3. A. See line 7.
4. B. See line 13.
5. C. See line 11. You can work out you would need a stove to boil the water in a saucepan to cook the egg.
6. B. See line 1. You can work out from the title 'Lunchtime' that the writer would eat an egg and lettuce roll for lunch.

Unit 5B page 17

1. A. put B. egg C. peel
2. A. chop B. boil C. knife
3. Answers will vary, e.g. cop, hop, lop, mop, pop, top.
4. peel
5. cut
6. mend
7. roll
8. 

9. break
10. into the roll
11. I boiled the egg.
12. She made an egg roll.

Unit 6A page 18

1. C. See line 5.
2. A. See lines 6–7.
3. C. See line 8.
4. A. See lines 8–10.
5. C. See lines 3–4. You can work out you need to start from the beginning and do everything again. It wouldn't make sense to do only one part over and over.
6. C. You can work out the picture is a chart that shows how many objects are needed for each number. This is the reason the number five has five ladybirds drawn next to it.

Unit 6B page 19

1. A. the B. fun C. nine
2. A. door B. pick C. four
3. Answers will vary, e.g. kick, lick, nick, sick, tick, wick.
4. again
5. neatly
6. tickle
7. shoe
8. 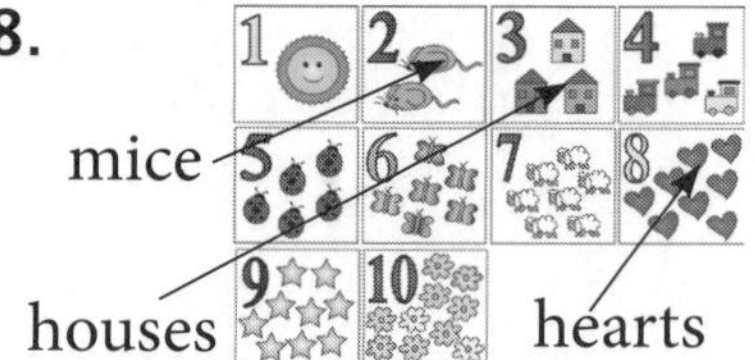

9. do
10. at the door
11. We said the poem.
12. We had fun.

Unit 7A page 20

1. C. See line 2.
2. B. See line 3.
3. C. See line 5.
4. A. See line 6.
5. C. See line 4. You can work out there are rules against having goats living inside units. It would not be healthy for Sam or for the family to have her living there with them.
6. B. You can work out that when Tom moves house and his goat is sold he won't see Sam any more.

Unit 7B page 21

1. A. buy B. miss C. grass
2. A. unit B. city C. soft

3. Answers will vary, e.g. boat, coat, moat, note, vote.
4. beard
5. shortly
6. soft
7. goat
8. 

9. miss
10. in the city
11. Our goat lives on a farm.
12. Goats eat anything.

Revision 1 pages 22–23

1. In one week Tom will be six years old. He ticks off the days on his calendar. There are still seven more days to wait. His birthday is on 4 March.
   He is having a party in his garden. He will have a birthday cake with candles. Everyone in his class is coming.
2. I fell over at school today. I cut my knee badly on a hard stone. My friend found the teacher. The teacher was kind to me. She put a bandage on my knee. I nearly cried but I stopped myself. Then she patted my head and said "What a brave girl."
3. 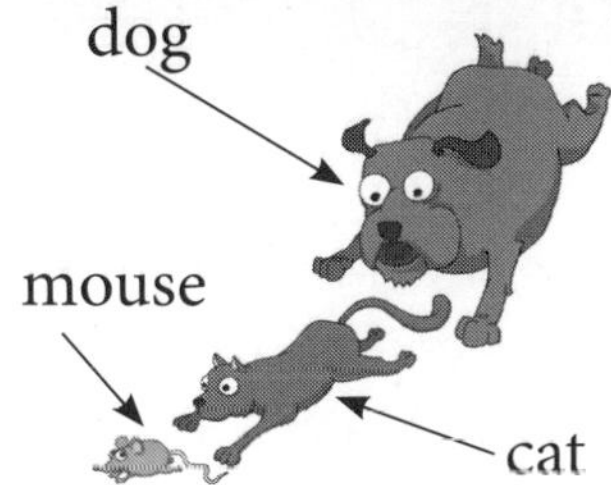

4. roll
5. pets
6. now
7. tiny
8. A. in the city B. on my cake C. in a bed
9. It is good to have a friend.

NAPLAN-style Reading Test 1 page 24

1. B. See lines 1–2.
2. A. See line 4.
3. C. See lines 4–5.
4. C. See lines 6–7.
5. C. See lines 3–4. You can work out that the goat is not a small pet. It is too big to live in Molly's home in the city where the garden is small.
6. B. See lines 4–5. You can work out the goat belonged to Molly's family because she refers to it as "our" goat.

NAPLAN-style Language Conventions Test 1 page 25

1. B.
2. house
3. B.
4. B.
5. C.
6. C.
7. in the city
8. C.

Unit 8A page 26

1. A. See line 3.
2. C. See line 4.
3. C. See line 5.
4. B. See line 2.
5. C. See lines 6–7. You can work out that as Bill had already been mean to Sally on the bus, she thought he might be mean to her again.
6. A. See lines 10–11. You can work out that Bill must like Sally as he always wants to sit next to her.

Unit 8B page 27

1. A. bus B. she C. said
2. A. school B. next C. hope
3. Answers will vary, e.g. bill, dill, fill, gill, hill, mill, pill, sill, till.
4. mean
5. near
6. went
7. wheels
8. 

9. was
10. in the morning
11. Are you sorry?
12. Do you go to school?

Unit 9A page 28

1. B. See lines 2–3.
2. C. See lines 3–4.
3. C. See lines 5–7.

Answers

4. A. See lines 5–7.
5. B. See line 8. You can work out the writer is a child because he or she has a bear of his or her own.
6. A. See the title and lines 5–7. You can work out that all the things the mum and dad buy are for a baby that hasn't arrived yet.

Unit 9B page 29

1. A. bear B. shed C. new
2. A. milk B. bottle C. pram
3. Answers will vary, e.g. bad, cad, fad, had, lad, mad, pad, sad.
4. already
5. old
6. later
7. bottle
8.

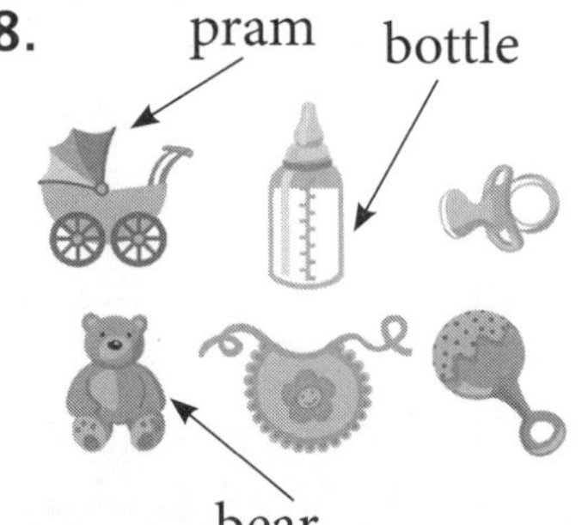

9. drink
10. last week
11. Will the baby cry?
12. Is the pram new?

Unit 10A page 30

1. A. See lines 2–3.
2. C. See lines 3–4.
3. C. See lines 4–6.
4. A. See lines 7–8.
5. B. See line 6. You can work out the best time to eat an apple is after a meal because that helps keep your teeth clean as well as it being healthy for you.
6. B. See lines 9–10. You can work that if apples keep you healthy you won't need to have a doctor visit very often.

Unit 10B page 31

1. A. box B. day C. you
2. A. bones B. teeth C. apple
3. Answers will vary, e.g. beat, feat, feet, heat, meat, meet, neat, peat, seat, teat.
4. clean
5. plenty
6. bad
7. box
8.

doctor
teeth
apple

9. eat
10. after dinner/a day
11. Do you eat an apple a day?
12. Are apples good for you?

Unit 11A page 32

1. C. See lines 3–4.
2. A. See line 5.
3. C. See lines 5–6.
4. A. See lines 7–8.
5. B. See lines 7–8. You can work out Dad kicks the ball so high it gets caught in the branches of the tree.
6. C. See lines 9–11. You can work out they won't have a ball to play with now it is out of reach because it is stuck in a tree.

Unit 11B page 33

1. A. boy B. man C. park
2. A. look B. tree C. ball
3. Answers will vary, e.g. call, fall, hall, mall, tall, wall.
4. stuck
5. ended
6. short
7. park
8.

9. kicks
10. this morning
11. I was upset when the ball got stuck.
12. Will you help get my ball?

Unit 12A page 34

1. B. See lines 2–3.
2. A. See line 5.
3. A. See lines 5–7.
4. B. See line 9.

Answers

5. C. See lines 3–4. You can work out the holes are already in the book when Kim reads it so it must have been made that way.
6. B. See lines 7–9. You can work out Kim thinks a caterpillar turning into a butterfly is like a magical trick as they are very different from each other.

Unit 12B page 35

1. A. fun B. very C. book
2. A. cocoon B. caterpillar C. butterfly
3. Answers will vary, e.g. cook, hook, look, nook, rook, sook, took.
4. holes
5. starving
6. spits
7. book/story
8. books Kim pages
9. eat
10. this morning
11. Is the story about a caterpillar?
12. Kim likes this story.

Unit 13A page 36

1. C. See line 3.
2. A. See line 4.
3. B. See lines 4–5.
4. A. See lines 7–8.
5. A. See lines 7–10. You can work out ladybirds live in fields and gardens because that is where they can find plenty of insects.
6. B. See lines 9–10. You can work out farmers would like having ladybirds in their crops because they save them from being eaten by insects.

Unit 13B page 37

1. A. red B. black C. like
2. A. head B. spots C. legs
3. Answers will vary, e.g. back, lack, pack, rack, sack, tack.
4. spots
5. tiny
6. like
7. insects
8.

9. like
10. all the time
11. How many legs does it have?
12. Do ladybirds eat plants?

Unit 14A page 38

1. B. See line 2.
2. C. See lines 4–5.
3. A. See line 6.
4. C. See lines 7–8.
5. B. See lines 6–7. You can work out he is a male dog because he is called Mr. Also the colour of his fur is brown so he is called Mr Brown.
6. A. See lines 3–4. You can work out the dog home is full of dogs. Mr Brown wants to be in a home where he feels special with his own family.

Unit 14B page 39

1. A. home B. ears C. love
2. A. brown B. will C. visit
3. Answers will vary, e.g. bogs, cogs, fogs, hogs, jogs, logs, togs.
4. sad
5. smooth
6. before
7. walks
8. ears face fur
9. has
10. very soon
11. I took Mr Brown home with me.
12. Does Mr Brown have floppy ears?

Unit 15A page 40

1. C. See line 2.
2. A. See line 4.
3. C. See lines 6–7.
4. A. See line 5.
5. B. You can work out that farmers pick the fruit when it is ripe, in autumn, so they can sell it then.

Answers

6. A. See lines 4–6. You can work out farmers would need to put their apples in boxes to carry them safely to market where they will be sold.

Unit 15B page 41

1. A. grow B. sold C. boxes
2. A. when B. apple C. pack
3. Answers will vary, e.g. back, hack, jack, lack, rack, sack, tack.
4. different
5. kind
6. few
7. apple
8. trees apples boxes
9. pick
10. in the autumn
11. Which is your favourite apple?
12. Do you like Granny Smiths?

Revision 2 pages 42–43

1. A ladybird is a small insect with a very small head. It has six legs and two pairs of wings. The top pair of wings are yellow, red or orange with black spots. Ladybirds eat insects that eat plants. Farmers like having ladybirds in their crops all the time. I wonder why?
2. I live in a home for dogs. I want to live in a home with a family. I have floppy ears, soft brown fur and a sad face. My name is Mr Brown. I love to go for walks. Please visit me very soon and then take me home with you. Will you?
3. pram bottle bear bib
4. mean
5. clean
6. small
7. hate
8. A. in the summer B. every night C. this morning
9. Do farmers like ladybirds?

NAPLAN-style Reading Test 2 page 44

1. C. See line 2.
2. B. See lines 3–4.
3. C. See lines 5–6.
4. A. See lines 7–8.
5. A. See lines 9–11. You can work out Mum thinks the spots mean Sali is getting measles or some other sickness. She says "Oh no!" because this adds another thing to make it a bad day for her (and Sali!).
6. B. You can work out that everything that happened added to Mum's bad day—she couldn't find the book she wanted; she fell and dropped her apples; she thought her daughter was getting sick. Several things went wrong.

NAPLAN-style Language Conventions Test 2 page 45

1. B.
2. insects
3. C.
4. dropped
5. C.
6. A.
7. After my bath
8. C.

Unit 16A page 46

1. C. See line 3.
2. C. See lines 6–7.
3. B. See line 4.
4. A. See lines 4–5.
5. C. See lines 6–10. You can work out Fred likes to watch the storm because he persuades Jarvis to watch it with him. He describes the storm with great interest.
6. B. See line 4. You can work out from what Jarvis says that he is scared by the storm.

Fred helps him to feel safer.

Unit 16B page 47

1. A. look B. stay C. that
2. A. sky B. loud C. watch
3. Answers will vary, e.g. bay, day, hay, may, pay, say.
4. lightning
5. noisy
6. under
7. thunder
8.

9. run
10. brightly
11. We watched the storm.
12. Ooh, watch out!

Unit 17A page 48

1. C. See line 2.
2. C. See lines 5–6.
3. A. See lines 7–8.
4. B. See lines 9–11.
5. B. See lines 3–6. You can work out the discs are the parts of the yoyo made from wood or plastic. This means they must be round.
6. A. See lines 9–11. You can work out that because yoyos have been played with for thousands of years, your grandparents could have played with them when they were children. This doesn't mean they did play with them—just that they could have.

Unit 17B page 49

1. A. yoyo B. two C. spin
2. A. make B. flat C. string
3. Answers will vary, e.g. bin, din, fin, pin, sin, tin, win.
4. flat/flat-sided
5. spin
6. loosely
7. yoyos
8.

9. spin
10. tightly
11. She has a yoyo.
12. Look at my yoyo spin!

Unit 18A page 50

1. A. See lines 2–3.
2. B. See line 2.
3. C. See lines 4–5.
4. B. See lines 6–8.
5. A. See lines 9–11. You can work out that since Aboriginal people painted the dots they would know best what stories they tell.
6. C. See lines 9–11. You can work out that the past is a long time. This means boomerangs have been in Australia for many, many years.

Unit 18B page 51

1. A. flat B. wood C. know
2. A. dots B. kangaroo C. boomerang
3. Answers will vary, e.g. bell, cell, dell, fell, hell, sell, well.
4. often
5. returns
6. pat
7. boomerang
8.

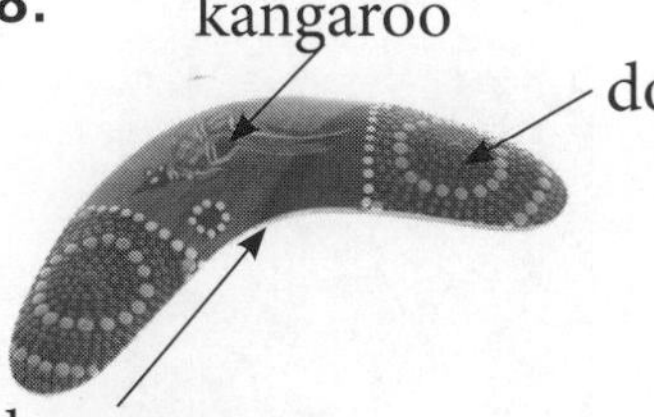

9. painted
10. quickly
11. Look out!
12. What a beautiful boomerang!

Unit 19A page 52

1. C. See line 3.
2. A. See line 5.
3. C. See line 8.
4. B. See lines 5–6.
5. A. You can work out it would help to know when to plant potatoes so the potato gets the right temperature for growing.
6. C. See lines 2–3. You can work out that since

the old potatoes must have shoots when you plant them, it must be the shoots that make the new potatoes grow.

Unit 19B page 53

1. A. cut B. dig C. soil
2. A. hole B. pull C. plants
3. Answers will vary, e.g. beep, deep, heap, jeep, leap, seep, weep.
4. lots
5. halves
6. plant
7. potatoes
8. plants

potatoes

9. grow
10. deeply
11. Dad planted some potatoes.
12. Look what I grew in my garden!

Unit 20A page 54

1. B. See line 2.
2. C. See line 4.
3. A. See lines 7–8.
4. C. See lines 9–11.
5. A. See lines 7–8. You can work out the wolf needs Red Riding Hood to go to her gran's for his plan to work. You can't tell what his plan is but you can work out Red Riding Hood thinks it isn't a plan she wants to be part of.
6. C. See lines 9–11. You can work out Red Riding Hood doesn't trust the wolf. She goes home where she knows she'll be safe.

Unit 20B page 55

1. A. wolf B. three C. home
2. A. said B. late/tale C. plan
3. Answers will vary, e.g. cast, fast, last, mast, vast.
4. today
5. fast
6. late
7. time
8. path wolf

Red Riding Hood

9. tricked
10. quickly
11. She went home.
12. She tricked me!

Unit 21A page 56

1. A. See line 3.
2. C. See lines 4–5.
3. A. See line 6.
4. B. See line 10.
5. A. See lines 3–5. You can work out koalas sleep in the day and the night because they are asleep most of the time—for about 20 hours per day.
6. B. See lines 10–11. You can work out that joeys grow bigger and so are ready to move out into the world.

Unit 21B page 57

1. A. fur B. ears C. milk
2. A. koala B. trees C. sleep
3. Answers will vary, e.g. bum, hum, mum, rum, sum.
4. cubs, joeys
5. remains
6. alive
7. Koalas
8. ears tree

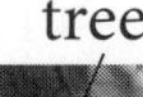

koala

9. sleep
10. slowly
11. The koala was asleep.
12. We must save the koalas!

Unit 22A page 58

1. C. See line 2.
2. B. See lines 4–5.
3. A. See lines 6–7.
4. C. See lines 8–9.
5. C. See lines 2–3. You

can work out that when the box drops on Juliet's foot it hurts her and makes her cry out.

6. A. See lines 8–10. You can work out that when the bruise under the nail shows it will look black and blue.

Unit 22B page 59

1. A. box B. big C. toe
2. A. hurt B. foot C. turn
3. Answers will vary, e.g. fight, light, night, right, sight, tight.
4. tripped
5. also
6. yelled
7. toe
8.

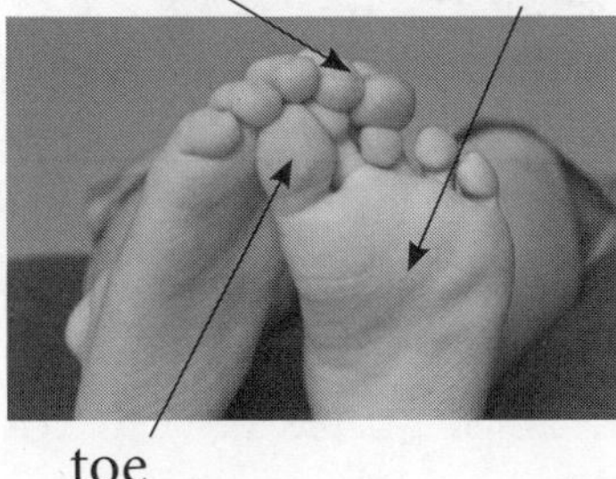

9. tripped
10. badly
11. Help!
12. Look out!

Revision 3 pages 60–61

1. "What's that noise, Fred?"
"It's thunder."
"Ooh, it's scary. It's so loud. Fido has run under the bed."
"Let's watch the sky from the window, Jarvis. Look! Above that roof. The lightning is flashing brightly. There will be more thunder in a minute," said Fred.
"Ooh, it's amazing! But please stay here with me, Fred."
2. A boomerang is a curved flat piece of wood. When you learn how, you can throw it so it comes back to you quickly. The Aboriginal people often painted animals such as kangaroos and lizards on their boomerangs. Some Aboriginal boomerangs have dot patterns that tell stories about the past.
3.

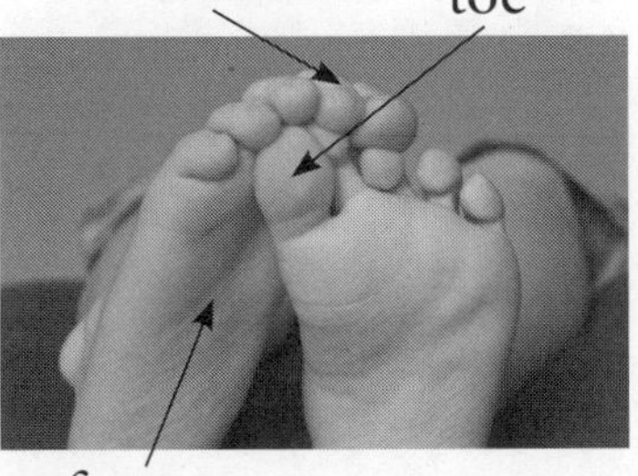

4. today
5. tiny
6. look
7. under
8. A. softly B. tightly C. greedily
9. B.

NAPLAN-style Reading Test 3 page 62

1. C. See line 3.
2. C. See lines 4–5.
3. B. See lines 5–7.
4. A. See lines 7–8.
5. A. See lines 7–9. You can work out Rosy hurt herself when she pulled the tooth quickly from her gum.
6. B. See lines 9–11. You can work out Rosy's dad is teasing her now that so much of her gum is showing.

NAPLAN-style Language Conventions Test 3 page 63

1. C.
2. morning
3. right
4. between
5. C.
6. B.
7. quickly
8. C.

Unit 23A page 64

1. B. See line 3.
2. C. See lines 4–5.
3. A. See lines 5–6.
4. B. See lines 6–7.
5. A. See lines 4–5. You can work out she is surprised because it is not what she is used to doing. It seems the custom must be different in Japan where Akiko comes from.
6. A., B., C. See the picture and lines 6–8. You can work out that as well as wearing hats outside, the children have their shoes on when they are outside. You can also see in the picture that on visits they take

their backpacks with them.

Unit 23B page 65

1. A. books B. school C. classroom
2. C.
3. Answers will vary, e.g. <u>U</u>ncle <u>U</u>gg, <u>s</u>tarted <u>s</u>chool
4. visits
5. began
6. indoors
7. Japan
8.

9. wear
10. badly
11. B.
12. C.

Unit 24A page 66

1. C. See lines 2–3.
2. A. See line 2.
3. A. See lines 5–6.
4. C. See line 8.
5. A. See lines 6–10. You can work out Pip was worried the title suggested the story would be sad and she didn't like that idea.
6. B., C. See lines 7–9. You can work out that Sad changed from being sad and not having an owner he liked to being happy and given a new name, and having Jack for his owner.

Unit 24B page 67

1. A. day B. end C. reads
2. A.
3. Answers will vary, e.g. <u>s</u>ad <u>s</u>tory, <u>n</u>ew <u>n</u>ame
4. everything
5. changed
6. happy
7. story
8.

9. gave
10. every day
11. B.
12. B.

Unit 25A page 68

1. A. See lines 2–3.
2. C. See lines 4–5.
3. A. See lines 8–9.
4. B. See lines 9–10.
5. B. See lines 10–11. You can work out that cities which are busy, crowded places need smooth, quick transport.
6. A. You can work out that newer forms of transport are faster and carry more goods and people than did the horse and cart.

Unit 25B page 69

1. A. buses B. cars C. planes
2. B.
3. Answers will vary, e.g. <u>t</u>rams <u>t</u>rains, <u>m</u>oves <u>m</u>ore
4. quickly
5. shift
6. ended
7. trams
8.

9. travel
10. smoothly, quickly
11. C.
12. B.

Unit 26A page 70

1. C. See line 3.
2. B. See line 4.
3. C. See line 7.
4. B. See line 8.
5. A. See lines 10–13. You can work out the bees are talking to people reading the poem who have the power to stop people who use sprays that harm them.
6. B. See line 12. You can work out the bees aren't interested in money or having a king but they do need to get people to stop the spraying that harms them.

Unit 26B page 71

1. A. hard B. bees C. busy
2. C.

Answers

3. Answers will vary, e.g. busy bees, We work, lays loads
4. no-one
5. many
6. lazy
7. bees
8.

9. ban
10. every day
11. C.
12. A.

Unit 27A page 72

1. B. See lines 2–3.
2. C. See lines 4–5.
3. B. See lines 6–7.
4. C. See line 9.
5. B. See lines 6–8. You can work out that baby possums are in their mothers' pouches because they need to be kept warm. If they are out of the pouch they will get too cold and could die.
6. A. See lines 5–6. You can work out the Wildlife Workers would need a lot of pouches for the many baby possums they have rescued.

Unit 27B page 73

1. A. hurt B. warm C. many
2. A.
3. Answers will vary, e.g. Wildlife Workers, need needles
4. hurt
5. save
6. help
7. Wildlife Workers
8.

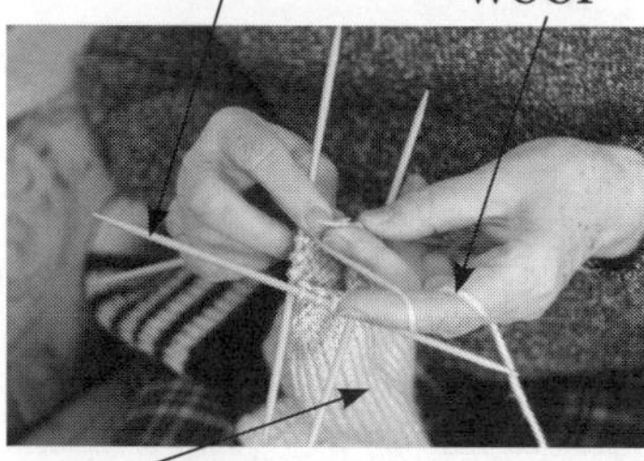

9. knit
10. right now
11. B.
12. A.

Unit 28A page 74

1. C. See lines 2–3.
2. B. See lines 4–6.
3. A. See line 7.
4. A. See lines 7–8.
5. C. You can work out that the class is making a museum to learn about things used in the past so they better understand that time.
6. C. See lines 9–11. You can work out that swimsuits covered more of the body as Grandpa's swimsuit went up to his neck.

Unit 28B page 75

1. A. old B. shed C. mask
2. B.
3. Answers will vary, e.g. sheep shed, striped swimsuit
4. museum
5. full
6. old
7. mask
8.

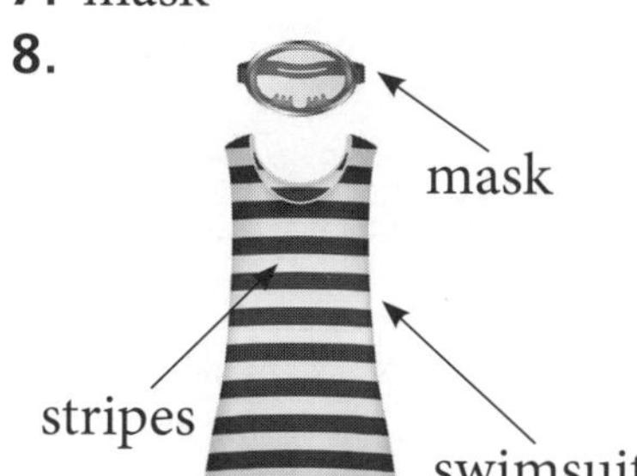

9. keep
10. this term
11. C.
12. B or C.

Unit 29A page 76

1. C. See line 3.
2. C. See line 6.
3. B. See lines 7–8.
4. A. See line 9.
5. A. See lines 4–5. You can work out that to travel a very long way in a very short time means it travels very quickly.
6. B. You can work out that since light travels faster than sound you will see lightning before you hear thunder.

Unit 29B page 77

1. A. light B. thunder C. sound
2. A.
3. Answers will vary, e.g. split second, can cause
4. travels
5. end

Answers

6. slow
7. sunscreen
8.

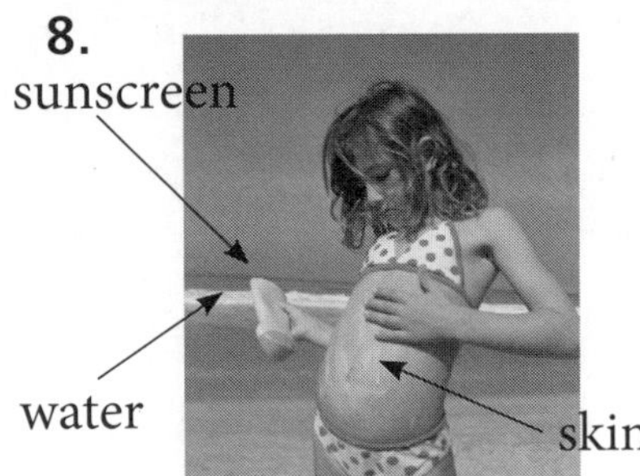

9. stops
10. faster than sound
11. A.
12. C.

Unit 30A page 78

1. C. See line 2.
2. C. See line 3.
3. B. See line 7.
4. A. See line 9.
5. B. See lines 3–5. You can work out that the last place the prince had seen the princess was in the palace because after that no-one had seen her—she was gone.
6. C. See lines 6–8. You can work out the birds are sad because they haven't any good news for the prince about the missing princess.

Unit 30B page 79

1. A. frogs B. prince C. birds
2. A.
3. Answers will vary, e.g. Prince Patrick, Princess Pearl
4. worried
5. then
6. after
7. princess
8.

9. looked
10. sadly
11. C.
12. A.

Revision 4 pages 80–81

1. Dear Uncle Ugg
   I have started school in Australia now. We keep our shoes on in the classroom! I have a backpack for my books. I wear a hat to keep off the sun when we play outside or go on visits. I miss Japan badly but I like it here too.
   Love
   Akiko
2. Right now the Wildlife Workers are helping baby possums. We rescue them when their mothers die or are hurt. Sadly, there are many of them. We must keep them warm when they are out of their mothers' pouches. Can you help us knit pouches for them? You will need needles and wool.
   The Wildlife Workers team
3.

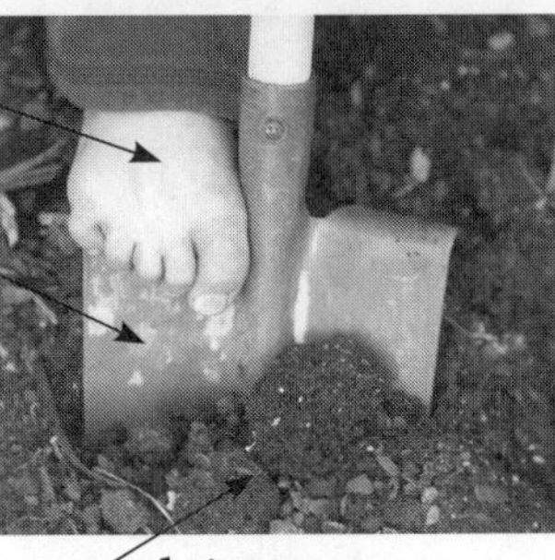

4. upset
5. harmed
6. still
7. light
8. A. badly B. quickly C. Sadly
9. Do animals leave tracks in the bush?

NAPLAN-style Reading Test 4 page 82

1. C. See line 3.
2. A. See line 6.
3. B. See line 7.
4. B. See line 8.
5. B. See lines 6, 9. You can work out that since Noah has to visit the country and the beach, he must live in the city.
6. C. You can work out that most of the things Noah likes to do are done outside.

NAPLAN-style Language Conventions Test 4 page 83

1. B.
2. like
3. big bike
4. most
5. A.
6. B.
7. around the city
8. C.

Spelling

3 Add nouns to label the pictures.

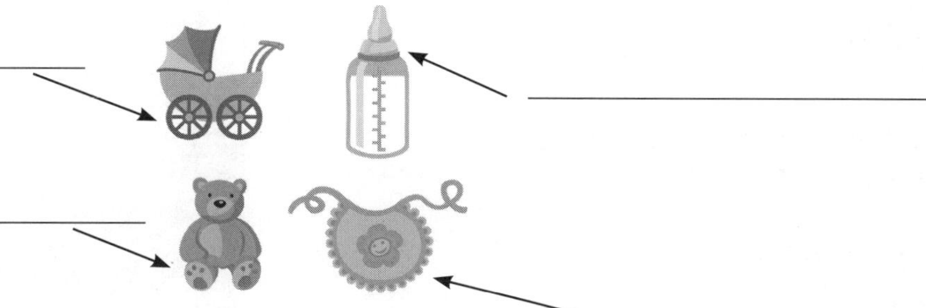

Vocabulary

4 Circle the word that means **unkind**.

She was mean to me yesterday.

5 Circle the word that means **not dirty**.

I have a clean pair of shoes.

6 Circle the word that has a similar meaning to **tiny**.

old new small

7 Cross out the word that does **not** belong.

like love hate

Grammar

8 Choose a prepositional phrase from the box to complete the sentences.

every night	in the summer	this morning

A I like to swim ______________________________.

B Dad reads me a story ______________________________.

C Mum cooked an apple pie ____________________ for our dinner.

Punctuation

9 Write this sentence correctly.

do farmers like ladybirds

____

NAPLAN-STYLE

2

READING TEST

Reading

Mum's bad day

Mum took a bus to the shops. She wanted to buy Dad a book about insects for his birthday. She couldn't find one. She bought some apples and put them in her basket. As she left the shop, she tripped and dropped her apples. Then, after my bath, Mum said 'Oh no! You have red spots on your tummy, Sali.'

1 How did Mum get to the shops?

A She walked.

B She rode her bike.

C She took the bus.

2 What did Mum want to buy for Dad?

A some apples

B a book about insects

C a basket

3 What did Mum buy?

A a book

B a basket and some apples

C some apples

4 What happened when Mum tripped?

A She dropped her basket of apples.

B She cried.

C She hurt her head.

5 Why does Mum say 'Oh no!'?

A She thinks red spots mean Sali is sick.

B She doesn't like spots.

C She thinks Sali stayed too long in the bath.

6 What made Mum's day a bad one?

A She tripped over.

B A few things went wrong.

C She lost her apples.

NAPLAN-STYLE

2

CONVENTIONS OF LANGUAGE TEST

Spelling

1 Which word is spelt correctly?

A aple **B** apple **C** applle

2 Find the spelling mistake and write the word correctly on the line.

Mum bought a book about insexts. ______________________________

3 Which word does **not** rhyme with **book**?

A cook **B** look **C** back

Vocabulary

4 Which word in the text means **let fall**?

____

5 Which word means the same as the underlined words?

Mum had a <u>very bad</u> day.

A nice **B** good **C** awful

Grammar

6 Which verb completes the sentence correctly?

Please ________________ the apples in my basket.

A put **B** puts **C** putting

7 Circle the words that tell **when** in this sentence.

After my bath, Mum said, 'Oh no!'

Punctuation

8 Which sentence is punctuated correctly?

A Did her mum have a bad day.

B did her mum have a bad day?

C Did her mum have a bad day?

Reading and Comprehension

The storm

'What's that noise, Fred?'

'It's thunder.'

'Ooh, it's scary. It's so loud. Fido has run under the bed.'

'Let's watch the sky from the window, Jarvis. Look! Above that roof. The lightning is flashing brightly. There will be more thunder in a minute,' said Fred.

'Ooh, it's amazing! But please stay here with me, Fred.'

1. What makes the noise?
   - **A** the lightning
   - **B** the dog
   - **C** the thunder

2. Who looks out of the window?
   - **A** Fred and Fido
   - **B** Jarvis and Fido
   - **C** Fred and Jarvis

3. What makes the thunder scary?
   - **A** It's amazing.
   - **B** It's very loud.
   - **C** It hurts you.

4. Who hides under the bed?
   - **A** Fido
   - **B** Jarvis
   - **C** Fred

5. What does Fred think about the storm?
   - **A** It is noisy.
   - **B** It is scary.
   - **C** It is good to watch.

6. Why does Jarvis ask Fred to stay with him?
   - **A** He likes Fred.
   - **B** He is afraid of the storm.
   - **C** He is afraid of Fido.

UNIT 16B

Spelling

1 Unscramble the letters to make words.

A kool ______

B yast ______

C atth ______

2 Unscramble the letters to make words.

A kys ______

B dlou ______

C chwat ______

3 Write words that rhyme with **stay**.

A _ _ _ **B** _ _ _ **C** _ _ _

Vocabulary

4 Which word from the text means **flash of light**?

______

5 Circle the word that has a similar meaning to **loud**.

quiet still noisy

6 Cross out the word that does **not** belong.

above under over

7 Add a word from the text to complete the sentence.

Did you hear the ______?

Grammar

8 Draw lines from the nouns to label the picture:

sky

roof

lightning

9 Choose a verb from the box to complete the sentence.

swept	run	chew

The dog has ______ under the bed

10 Write an adverb from the text to tell **how**.

Did you see the lightning flash

______?

Punctuation

A sentence begins with a capital letter. If the sentence expresses strong feelings, it ends with an exclamation mark.

Write each sentence correctly.

11 we watched the storm

______

12 ooh, watch out

______

Reading and Comprehension

The yoyo

A yoyo is a toy. It is made from two round, flat-sided pieces of wood or plastic. String is wound tightly between these two discs. The string can make the yoyo spin up and down. Boys and girls have played with yoyos for thousands (1000s) of years.

1 What is a yoyo?

- A two discs
- B a string
- C a toy

2 What is wound between the two discs?

- A wood
- B plastic
- C string

3 How does the yoyo spin?

- A up and down
- B over and over
- C round and about

4 For how long have yoyos been used?

- A hundreds (100s) of years
- B thousands (1000s) of years
- C millions (1 000 000s) of years

5 What shape are the discs?

- A square
- B round
- C oval

6 Could your grandparents have played with yoyos?

- A yes
- B maybe
- C no

Spelling

1 Unscramble the letters to make words.

A oyoy ____________

B wto ____________

C pins ____________

2 Unscramble the letters to make words.

A kmae ____________

B altf ____________

C ringst ____________

3 Write words that rhyme with **spin**.

A ______ B ______ C ______

Vocabulary

4 Which word from the text means **smooth**?

____

5 Circle the word that has a similar meaning to **make turn around fast**.

____

6 Cross out the word that does **not** belong.

firmly loosely tightly

7 Add a word from the text to complete the sentence.

We had fun playing with our

____________.

Grammar

8 Draw lines from the nouns to label the picture:

yoyo

string

girl

9 Choose a verb from the box to complete the sentence.

make	spin	goes

Yoyos can ____________ up and down.

10 Write an adverb from the text to tell **how**.

The string is wound

____________.

Punctuation

A sentence begins with a capital letter. If the sentence expresses strong feelings, it ends with an exclamation mark.

Write each sentence correctly.

11 she has a yoyo

____

12 look at my yoyo spin

____

Reading and Comprehension

What is a boomerang?

A boomerang is a curved flat piece of wood. When you learn how, you can throw it so it comes back to you quickly. The Aboriginal people often painted animals such as kangaroos and lizards on their boomerangs. Some Aboriginal boomerangs have dot patterns that tell stories about the past.

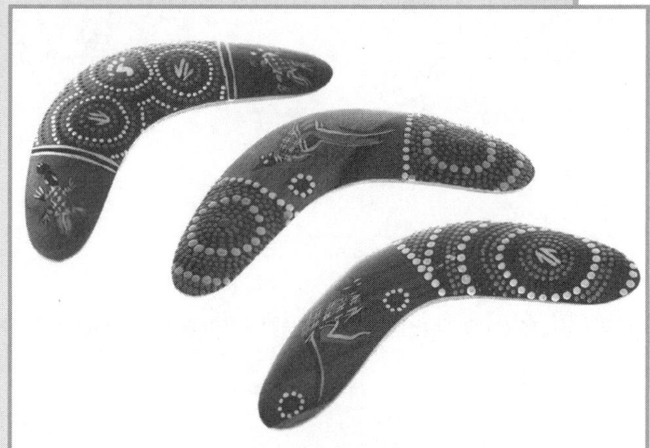

1. What is a boomerang made from?
   - **A** wood
   - **B** rock
   - **C** paint

2. What shape is a boomerang?
   - **A** square
   - **B** curved
   - **C** round

3. If you throw a boomerang the right way
   - **A** it will get lost.
   - **B** it will not come back.
   - **C** it will come back.

4. What are often painted on Aboriginal boomerangs?
   - **A** food
   - **B** animals
   - **C** trees

5. Who would best know about the stories made by the dots?
   - **A** the Aboriginal people
   - **B** the writer of the text
   - **C** the kangaroos

6. How long have there been boomerangs in Australia?
   - **A** a few years
   - **B** a few months
   - **C** many, many years

Spelling

1 Unscramble the letters to make words.

A talf ____

B oowd ____

C owkn ____

2 Unscramble the letters to make words.

A tosd ____

B angakoor ____

C angerboom ____

3 Write words that rhyme with **tell**.

A ____ B ____ C ____

Vocabulary

4 Which word from the text means **many times**?

____

5 Circle the word that has a similar meaning to **comes back**.

goes moves returns

6 Cross out the word that does **not** belong.

hurl throw pat

7 Add a word from the text to complete the sentence.

Can you throw a

____.

Grammar

8 Draw lines from the nouns to label the picture:

boomerang

kangaroo

dots

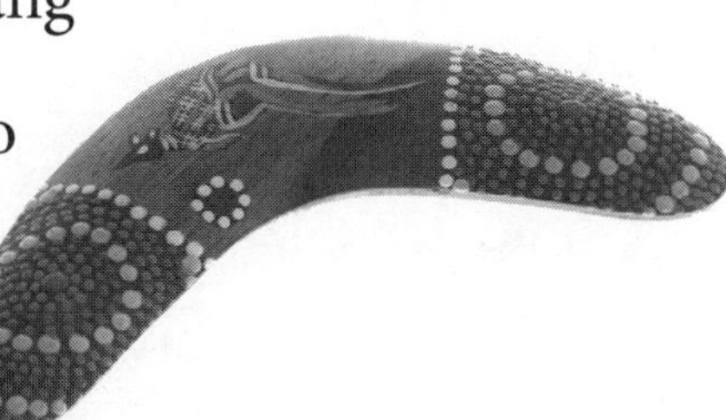

9 Choose a verb from the box to complete the sentence.

sent	know	painted

I ____

a pattern of dots.

10 Write an adverb from the text to tell **how**.

The boomerang came back to me

____.

Punctuation

A sentence begins with a capital letter. If the sentence expresses strong feelings, it ends with an exclamation mark.

Write each sentence correctly.

11 Look out

____

12 what a beautiful boomerang

____

____

Reading and Comprehension

How to grow potatoes easily

1. Take two potatoes that are sprouting shoots.
2. Cut the potatoes in half.
3. Dig a hole in the soil.
4. Plant the halves deeply and keep watered.
5. Watch green plants grow and flower.
6. After the flowers die, pull up the plants.
7. You will have lots of potatoes!

1 What do potatoes sprout?

A soil

B leaves

C shoots

2 What do you dig in the soil?

A a hole

B a plant

C a potato

3 What colour plants grow from the soil?

A brown

B white

C green

4 Where do you plant the halved potatoes?

A in a bucket

B in soil

C in water

5 What other information would help?

A the best time of year for planting

B the colour of potatoes

C the number of potatoes you will grow

6 What do the new potatoes grow from?

A the soil

B the leaves on the plants

C the shoots on the old potatoes

Spelling

1 Unscramble the letters to make words.

A tuc ....

B igd ....

C ilos ....

2 Unscramble the letters to make words.

A hloe ....

B llup ....

C ntsapl ....

3 Write words that rhyme with **keep**.

A _ _ _ _ B _ _ _ _ C _ _ _ _

Vocabulary

4 Which word from the text means **plenty**?

....

5 Circle the word that has a similar meaning to **two equal parts**.

two some halves

6 Cross out the word that does **not** belong.

cut slice plant

7 Add a word from the text to complete the sentence.

Anyone can grow

.... easily.

Grammar

8 Draw lines from the nouns to label the picture:

potatoes

plants

9 Choose a verb from the box to complete the sentence.

saw	grow	dug

It is easy to .... potatoes.

10 Write an adverb from the text to tell **how**.

You need to plant the potato halves

.... in the soil.

Punctuation

Write each sentence correctly.

11 dad planted some potatoes

....

....

12 look what I grew in my garden

....

....

Reading and Comprehension

A fairy tale

'Hello Red Riding Hood,' said the wolf.

'Hello Mr Wolf. Do you have the time?'

'It's half past three.'

'Oh dear. I'm late. I'd better go home again.'

'You mustn't! You said you'd see your gran today,' said the wolf who had a plan.

'Tricked you,' said Red Riding Hood and ran quickly back down the path to her home.

1. Who is the wolf talking to?
   - **A** himself
   - **B** Red Riding Hood
   - **C** Gran
2. What time is it in the fairy tale?
   - **A** half past one
   - **B** two o'clock
   - **C** half past three
3. When did Red Riding Hood say she'd see her gran?
   - **A** today
   - **B** yesterday
   - **C** tomorrow
4. Where does Red Riding Hood go at the end of the story?
   - **A** to her gran's house
   - **B** to the wolf's house
   - **C** to her own house
5. Why does the wolf say, 'You mustn't!'?
   - **A** He has a plan that won't work if she goes home.
   - **B** He wants to have a picnic with her.
   - **C** He is bossy.
6. Red Riding Hood tricks the wolf because
   - **A** she likes him.
   - **B** she is always playing tricks.
   - **C** she is afraid he might have a trick of his own.

Spelling

1 Unscramble the letters to make words.

A wflo ______

B reeth ______

C hmoe ______

2 Unscramble the letters to make words.

A dsai ______

B atel ______

C npal ______

3 Write words that rhyme with **past**.

A ____ B ____ C ____

Vocabulary

4 Which word from the text means **on this day**?

______

5 Circle the word that has a similar meaning to **quickly**.

soon hard fast

6 Cross out the word that does **not** belong.

early before late

7 Add a word from the text to complete the sentence.

Could you tell me the ______ please?

Grammar

8 Draw lines from the nouns to label the picture:

Red Riding Hood wolf path

9 Choose a verb from the box to complete the sentence.

trap	tricked	tried

Red Riding Hood ______ the wolf.

10 Write an adverb from the text to tell **how**.

Red Riding Hood ran home ______.

Punctuation

Write each sentence correctly.

11 she went home

______

12 she tricked me

______

Reading and Comprehension

Koalas

Koalas live in trees in bushland. They eat gum leaves. They sleep most of the day (about 20 hours). Their babies, called cubs or joeys, are about 2 cm long when born. They move slowly into the mother's pouch where they can drink milk. Their ears and fur grow while they are in the pouch.

1. What do koalas eat?
   - **A** gum leaves
   - **B** bushland
   - **C** pouches

2. About how many hours does a koala sleep in a day?
   - **A** 6
   - **B** 2
   - **C** 20

3. How long are joeys when they are born?
   - **A** 2 cm
   - **B** 4 cm
   - **C** 6 cm

4. What happens to joeys in the pouch?
   - **A** They feed on gum leaves.
   - **B** They grow ears and fur.
   - **C** They stay the same size.

5. Which statement is true?
   - **A** Koalas sleep in the day and the night.
   - **B** Koalas only sleep in the day.
   - **C** Koalas only sleep at night.

6. Why does a joey leave the pouch?
   - **A** It is hungry.
   - **B** It is ready to live outside the pouch.
   - **C** It wants to find more milk.

UNIT 21B

Spelling

1 Unscramble the letters to make words.

A ruf ____________

B reas ____________

C lkim ____________

2 Unscramble the letters to make words.

A kolaa ____________

B stree ____________

C eepsl ____________

3 Write words that rhyme with **gum**.

A ___ ___ ___ B ___ ___ ___ C ___ ___ ___

Vocabulary

4 Which words from the text mean **koalas' babies**?

____

5 Circle the word that has a similar meaning to **stays**.

goes comes remains

6 Cross out the word that does **not** belong.

about around alive

7 Add a word from the text to complete the sentence.

____

sleep a lot.

Grammar

8 Draw lines from the nouns to label the picture:

koala ears tree

9 Choose a verb from the box to complete the sentence.

grows climbs sleep

Koalas ____________
for about 20 hours a day.

10 Write an adverb from the text to tell **how**.

The joey moved ____________
into its mother's pouch.

Punctuation

Write each sentence correctly.

11 the koala was asleep

____

____

12 we must save the koalas

____

____

Reading and Comprehension

Ouch!

I dropped a box on my foot. Ouch! Then I tripped over a stone and stubbed the big toe on my right foot too. It hurt a lot. I cried a little bit. Dad said, 'The toenail on your big toe is bruised badly. It might turn black and blue, Juliet!'

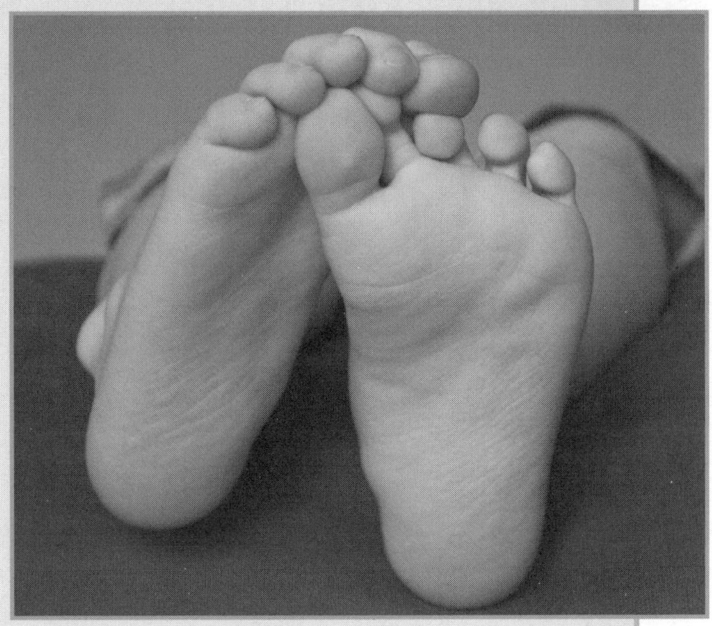

1 What did Juliet drop?

- **A** a nail
- **B** a foot
- **C** a box

2 What did Juliet stub?

- **A** her foot
- **B** her big toe
- **C** her other foot

3 How much did Juliet cry?

- **A** a little bit
- **B** a lot
- **C** not at all

4 What did Juliet's dad say was bruised?

- **A** the sole of her foot
- **B** her toes
- **C** the toenail on her big toe

5 Why does Juliet say 'Ouch!'?

- **A** because she wants her dad to hear
- **B** because she likes the sound of the word
- **C** because her foot hurt

6 Why would Juliet's toenail change colour?

- **A** The bruise would show through her toenail.
- **B** Her dad would paint it black and blue.
- **C** Her tears would make her toenail darker.

Spelling

1 Unscramble the letters to make words.

A xob ____

B gbi ____

C eot ____

2 Unscramble the letters to make words.

A htur ____

B ootf ____

C trun ____

3 Write words that rhyme with **might**.

A ____ B ____ C ____

Vocabulary

4 Which word from the text means **fell over**?

____

5 Circle the word that has a similar meaning to **too**.

again also always

6 Cross out the word that does **not** belong.

cried sobbed yelled

7 Add a word from the text to complete the sentence.

Did you know I stubbed my

____?

Grammar

8 Draw lines from the nouns to label the picture:

foot

toe

toenail

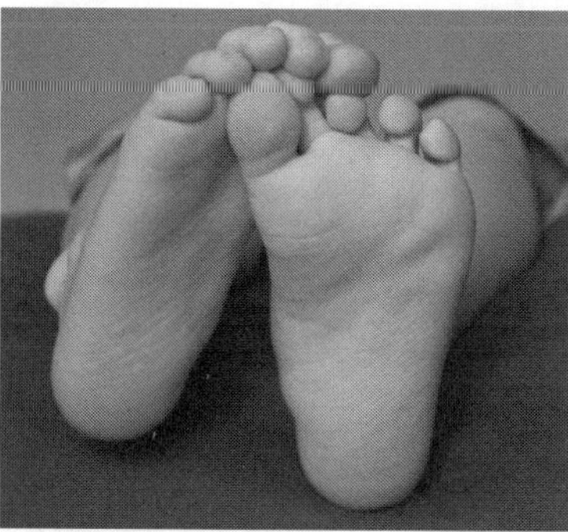

9 Choose a verb from the box to complete the sentence.

trips	tripped	fall

My foot was hurt when I

____.

10 Write an adverb from the text to tell **how**.

My big toe was bruised very

____

____.

Punctuation

Write each sentence correctly.

11 help

____

12 look out

____

Reading and Comprehension

1 Choose a word from the box to go in each space.

loud	bed	noise	stay	roof	window	brightly

'What's that ______________________, Fred?'

'It's thunder.'

'Ooh, it's scary. It's so ______________________. Fido has run under the ______________________.'

'Let's watch the sky from the ______________________, Jarvis.

Look! Above that ______________________. The lightning is flashing ______________________. There will be more thunder in a minute,' said Fred.

'Ooh, it's amazing! But please ______________________ here with me, Fred.'

2 Choose a word from the box to go in each space.

quickly	dot	wood	animals	throw	past	boomerangs

A boomerang is a curved flat piece of ______________________.

When you learn how, you can ______________________ it so it comes back to you ______________________. The Aboriginal people often painted ______________________ such as kangaroos and lizards on their ______________________. Some Aboriginal boomerangs have ______________________ patterns that tell stories about the ______________________.

Spelling

3 Add nouns to label the picture.

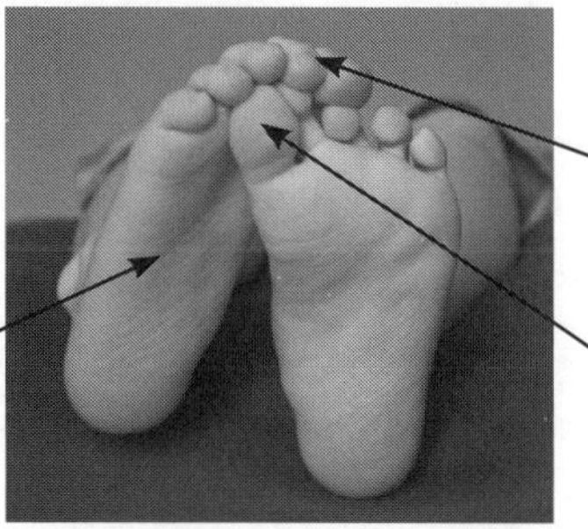

______________________ ______________________ ______________________

Vocabulary

4 Circle the word that means **on this day**.

tomorrow yesterday today

5 Circle the word that means **little**.

wide long tiny

6 Circle the word that has a similar meaning to **watch**.

hear look know

7 Cross out the word that does **not** belong.

under above over

Grammar

8 Choose an adverb from the box to complete each sentence.

tightly	greedily	softly

A I spoke ______________________ so only my friend could hear me.

B Hold my hand ______________________, please.

C He ______________________ ate everyone's food.

Punctuation

9 Which sentence is punctuated correctly?

A move away at once?

B Move away at once!

C Move away at once.

Reading

A gap

That girl in the picture is me, Rosy. I am six years old. You can see I am holding a tiny white tooth. My tooth was wobbly for a few weeks. This morning I pulled it quickly out of my gum. Ouch! Now there is a gap between my teeth. Dad calls me Gummy!

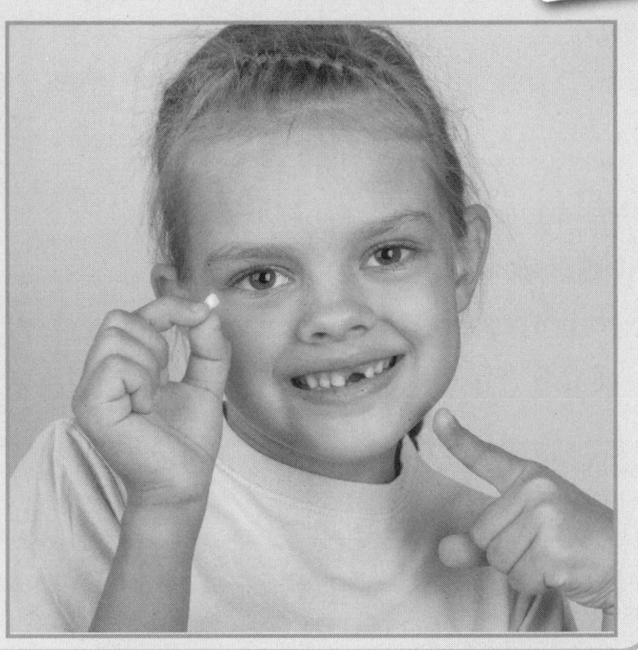

1 How old is Rosy?

- **A** four
- **B** five
- **C** six

2 What is Rosy holding?

- **A** a gum
- **B** a gap
- **C** a tooth

3 For how long was Rosy's tooth wobbly?

- **A** a few days
- **B** a few weeks
- **C** a long time

4 How did the tooth come out?

- **A** Rosy pulled it out.
- **B** It fell out.
- **C** Rosy's dad pulled it out.

5 Why does Rosy say 'Ouch!'?

- **A** because she hurt herself
- **B** because she always says it
- **C** because her dad calls her Gummy

6 Why does Rosy's dad call her Gummy?

- **A** It rhymes with mummy.
- **B** He can see more of Rosy's gum now.
- **C** He wants to be unkind.

NAPLAN-STYLE

3

CONVENTIONS OF LANGUAGE TEST

Spelling

1 Which word is spelt correctly?

A toothe   B toth   C tooth

2 Find the spelling mistake and write the word correctly on the line.

This morrning I hurt myself. ______________________________

3 Which word rhymes with **white**?

right   went   which

Vocabulary

4 Which word means **in the middle of**?

between   after   before

5 Which word means the same as the underlined word?

I yanked out my tooth.

A planted   B pushed   C pulled

Grammar

6 Which verb completes the sentence correctly?

I think there ______________________ a gap where my tooth was.

A were   B is   C was

7 Circle the word that tells **how** in this sentence.

My tooth was pulled out quickly.

Punctuation

8 Which sentence is punctuated correctly?

A Ouch.

B Ouch?

C Ouch!

Reading and Comprehension

Letter home

Dear Uncle Ugg

I have started school in Australia now. We keep our shoes on in the classroom! I have a backpack for my books. I wear a hat to keep off the sun when we play outside or go on visits. I miss Japan badly but I like it here too.

Love
Akiko

1. Where does Akiko go to school?
   - **A** Japan
   - **B** Australia
   - **C** Tokyo

2. What do the children keep on in the classroom?
   - **A** hats
   - **B** backpacks
   - **C** shoes

3. What does Akiko keep in her backpack?
   - **A** books
   - **B** shoes
   - **C** hats

4. Where do the children wear hats?
   - **A** in the classroom
   - **B** outside
   - **C** in Japan

5. Why is Akiko surprised to wear shoes in the classroom?
   - **A** She didn't wear shoes inside in Japan.
   - **B** She wears shoes everywhere she goes.
   - **C** She dislikes shoes.

6. What do children wear when they go on visits? Choose all that apply.
   - **A** hats
   - **B** backpacks
   - **C** shoes

Spelling

1 Unscramble the letters to make words.

A ookbs ....

B oolsch ....

C rmooclssa ....

2 Which word is spelt correctly?

A shoos

B shose

C shoes

3 Find two words next to each other in the text that begin with the same sound.

....

Vocabulary

4 Which word from the text means **goes to see people or places**?

....

5 Circle the word that has a similar meaning to **started**.

ended began stopped

6 Cross out the word that does **not** belong.

outside indoors outdoors

7 Add a word from the text to complete the sentence.

Uncle Ugg lives in

....

Grammar

8 Draw lines from the nouns to label the picture:

shoe

hat

backpack

9 Choose a verb from the box to complete the sentence.

want	wear	show

We .... hats when we go outside.

10 Write an adverb from the text to tell **how**.

Akiko misses Japan

....

Punctuation

11 Which sentence is punctuated correctly?

A Akiko likes going to school in Australia?

B Akiko likes going to school in Australia.

C Akiko likes going to school in Australia!

12 Which sentence is punctuated correctly?

A Would you like to visit Japan!

B would you like to visit Japan?

C Would you like to visit Japan?

Reading and Comprehension

Sad, the dog

Every day we sit on the floor and our teacher reads us a story. Today the story was by an Australian writer. It was called *Sad, the Dog* by Sandy Fussell. I wasn't sure I would like it. It was a sad story at first but then Sad's new owner, Jack, gave Sad a new name—Lucky. Everything changed and by the end I loved the story!

by Pip

1 How often does the teacher read the class a story?

- **A** every minute
- **B** every hour
- **C** every day

2 Where do the children sit?

- **A** on the floor
- **B** on the chairs
- **C** at their desks

3 What is the first name of the writer of the story?

- **A** Sandy
- **B** Pip
- **C** Jack

4 What is the name of Sad's new owner?

- **A** Pip
- **B** Sandy
- **C** Jack

5 Why wasn't Pip sure if she'd like the story?

- **A** It sounded sad.
- **B** It sounded happy.
- **C** She didn't like dogs.

6 What changed in the story? Choose all that apply.

- **A** Sad got a new kennel.
- **B** Sad got a new owner.
- **C** Sad got a new name.

UNIT 24B

Spelling

1 Unscramble the letters to make words.

A yda ....

B den ....

C seadr ....

2 Which word is spelt correctly?

A today

B twoday

C tooday

3 Find two words next to each other in the text that begin with the same sound.

....

Vocabulary

4 Which word from the text means **all things**?

....

5 Circle the word that has a similar meaning to **became different**.

stopped started changed

6 Cross out the word that does **not** belong.

sad happy unhappy

7 Add a word from the text to complete the sentence.

Which .... will the teacher read today?

Grammar

8 Draw lines from the nouns to label the picture:

teacher

floor

9 Choose a verb from the box to complete the sentence.

showed	gave	sent

Jack .... Sad a new name.

10 Write an adverb from the text to tell **when**.

We hear a story ....

Punctuation

11 Which sentence is punctuated correctly?

A Would you like to hear a story.

B Would you like to hear a story?

C Would you like to hear a story!

12 Which sentence is punctuated correctly?

A be quiet at once!

B Be quiet at once!

C Be quiet at once.

Reading and Comprehension

Transport

Transport is used to move people and goods from one place to another. Long ago people used horses and carts for transport. Later they began to use buses, trams, trains, cars and planes. Today many cities are using light rail. Light rail is like a tram but it moves more smoothly and more quickly.

1. What does transport move?
   - **A** people and goods
   - **B** cars and planes
   - **C** horses and carts

2. When did people use horses and carts?
   - **A** today
   - **B** later
   - **C** long ago

3. What are many cities using today?
   - **A** light rail
   - **B** horses and carts
   - **C** trams

4. What is light rail like?
   - **A** a train
   - **B** a tram
   - **C** a plane

5. Why are many cities using light rail?
   - **A** It looks good.
   - **B** It moves quickly and smoothly.
   - **C** It is cheap.

6. Has transport got better over time?
   - **A** yes
   - **B** maybe
   - **C** no

UNIT 25B

Spelling

1 Unscramble the letters to make words.

A bssue ....

B cras ....

C palnse ....

2 Which word is spelt correctly?

A trane

B train

C traine

3 Find two words next to each other in the text that begin with the same sound.

....

Vocabulary

4 Which word from the text means **very fast**?

....

5 Circle the word that has a similar meaning to **move**.

did shift stop

6 Cross out the word that does **not** belong.

started ended began

7 Add a word from the text to complete the sentence.

Light rail moves more quickly than

....

Grammar

8 Draw lines from the nouns to label the picture:

horse

cart

people

9 Choose a verb from the box to complete the sentence.

travel	goes	rode

My grandpa used to .... to town by horse and cart.

10 Write adverbs from the text to tell **how**.

Light rail moves ....

and ....

Punctuation

11 Which sentence is punctuated correctly?

A Have you ever been in a plane.

B have you ever been in a plane?

C Have you ever been in a plane?

12 Which sentence is punctuated correctly?

A my dad's grandpa had a horse and cart.

B My dad's grandpa had a horse and cart.

C My dad's grandpa had a horse and cart?

Reading and Comprehension

Busy bees

We are busy bees.
We work hard every day.
We catch pollen with our knees
but don't get any pay.

We are busy bees.
We make lots of honey.
Our queen lays loads of eggs
but no-one pays her money.

We have a deal for you.
It won't cost you a thing.
Just ban the sprays that harm us
And we'll make you our king.

1. When do the bees work hard?
   - **A** at night
   - **B** on some days
   - **C** every day

2. What do the bees catch on their knees?
   - **A** a cold
   - **B** pollen
   - **C** spray

3. What do the busy bees make?
   - **A** pollen
   - **B** money
   - **C** honey

4. Who lays the eggs?
   - **A** the king
   - **B** the queen
   - **C** the busy bees

5. 'We have a deal for you.' Who is the deal for?
   - **A** people
   - **B** other bees
   - **C** kings and queens

6. Why do the bees want to make a deal?
   - **A** to make money
   - **B** to stop the harmful spraying
   - **C** to get a new king

UNIT 26B

Spelling

1 Unscramble the letters to make words.

A dhar ....

B ebes ....

C ybus ....

2 Which word is spelt correctly?

A kneez

B knes

C knees

3 Find two words next to each other in the text that begin with the same sound.

....

Vocabulary

4 Which word from the text means **nobody**?

....

5 Circle the word that has a similar meaning to **lots**.

some many none

6 Cross out the word that does **not** belong.

busy lazy hard-working

7 Add a word from the text to complete the sentence.

Honey comes from ....

Grammar

8 Draw lines from the nouns to label the picture:

bee

pollen

9 Choose a verb from the box to complete the sentence.

stops	ban	ends

Please .... the sprays that harm the bees.

10 Write an adverb from the text to tell **when**.

Bees work hard

....

Punctuation

11 Which sentence is punctuated correctly?

A do you like honey?

B Do you like honey

C Do you like honey?

12 Which sentence is punctuated correctly?

A Ban the sprays!

B ban the sprays

C Ban the sprays?

Reading and Comprehension

Can you help us?

Right now the Wildlife Workers are helping baby possums. We rescue them when their mothers die or are hurt. Sadly, there are many of them. We must keep them warm when they are out of their mothers' pouches. Can you help us knit pouches for them? You will need needles and wool.

The Wildlife Workers

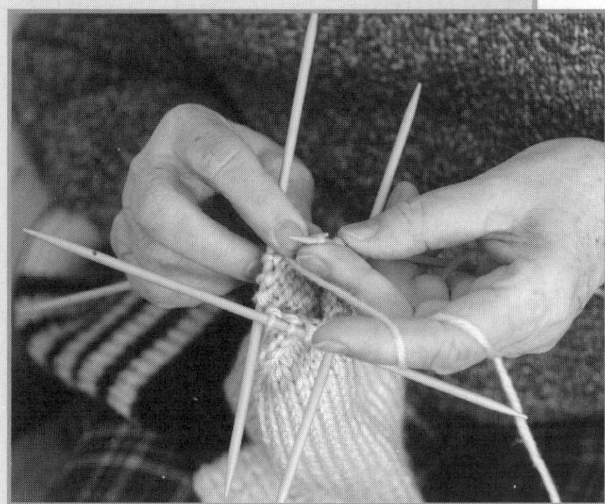

1. Who are the Wildlife Workers helping right now?
   - **A** people
   - **B** baby possums
   - **C** possums

2. What has happened to the mothers?
   - **A** They ran away.
   - **B** They lost their milk.
   - **C** They died or were hurt.

3. How must the baby possums be kept?
   - **A** cool
   - **B** warm
   - **C** happy

4. What can you do to help?
   - **A** Phone the Wildlife Workers.
   - **B** Buy needles and wool.
   - **C** Knit pouches.

5. Why do the babies need to be kept warm?
   - **A** They are lost.
   - **B** They get too cold outside the pouch.
   - **C** It is winter-time.

6. Why are people asked to knit pouches for the Wildlife Workers?
   - **A** They don't have enough.
   - **B** They look pretty.
   - **C** They are easy to knit.

Spelling

1 Unscramble the letters to make words.

A rthu ______

B wrma ______

C yman ______

2 Which word is spelt correctly?

A possum

B posum

C possumm

3 Find two words next to each other in the text that begin with the same sound.

______

Vocabulary

4 Which word from the text means **harm**?

______

5 Circle the word that has a similar meaning to **rescue**.

harm keep save

6 Cross out the word that does **not** belong.

help harm hurt

7 Add words from the text to complete the sentence.

You can help the ______ save the lives of wild animals.

Grammar

8 Draw lines from the nouns to label the picture:

needles

wool

pouch

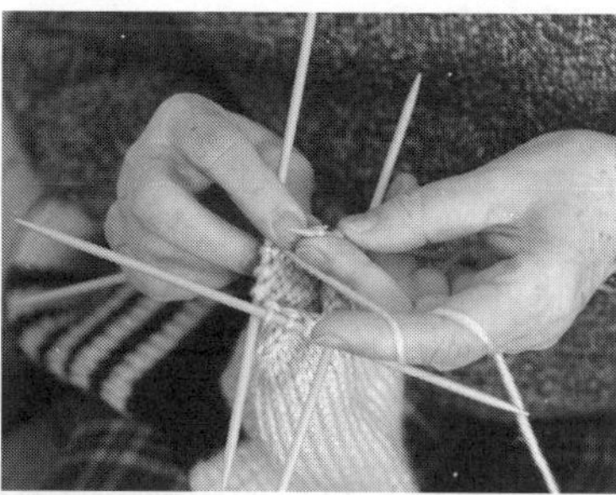

9 Choose a verb from the box to complete the sentence.

builds help knit

Can you ______ us a possum pouch please?

10 Write an adverb from the text to tell **when**.

The baby possums are being helped ______.

Punctuation

11 Which sentence is punctuated correctly?

A we rescued a baby possum

B We rescued a baby possum.

C We rescued a baby possum?

12 Which sentence is punctuated correctly?

A My friend knitted some pouches for the baby possums.

B my friend knitted some pouches for the baby possums.

C My friend knitted some pouches for the baby possums?

Reading and Comprehension

Our museum

Our class is making a museum in an old sheep shed this term. It is full of things people used in the past. My dad gave us his old box camera. Grandpa gave us his old striped swimsuit and his snorkel mask. Did you know men's swimsuits used to go up to their necks?

1. What is the class making?
   - **A** a shed
   - **B** a swimsuit
   - **C** a museum

2. The things in the museum are from
   - **A** now.
   - **B** the past.
   - **C** next year.

3. What kind of camera is in the museum?
   - **A** box
   - **B** new
   - **C** modern

4. What did Grandpa give to the museum?
   - **A** a swimsuit
   - **B** a camera
   - **C** a shed

5. Why is the class making a museum?
   - **A** to fill up the shed
   - **B** to learn more about cameras
   - **C** to learn more about the past

6. In the past swimsuits covered .... of the body.
   - **A** all
   - **B** less
   - **C** more

Spelling

1 Unscramble the letters to make words.

A dlo ____________

B desh ____________

C kmas ____________

2 Which word is spelt correctly?

A peeple

B people

C peaple

3 Find two words next to each other in the text that begin with the same sound.

____________ ____________ ____________

Vocabulary

4 Which word from the text means **a building where things are kept for people to visit**?

____

5 Circle the word that has a similar meaning to **filled up**.

wide full thick

6 Cross out the word that does **not** belong.

new unused old

7 Add a word from the text to complete the sentence.

Grandpa gave us the ____________ he wore to go snorkelling.

Grammar

8 Draw lines from the nouns to label the picture:

mask

swimsuit

stripes

9 Choose a verb from the box to complete the sentence.

wants	sends	keep

We ____________ things from the past in our museum.

10 Write an adverb from the text to tell **when**.

Our class is making a museum

____________.

Punctuation

11 Which sentence is punctuated correctly?

A Is your class making a museum

B Is your class making a museum!

C Is your class making a museum?

12 Which sentence is punctuated correctly?

A my sister wants to see our museum

B My sister wants to see our museum.

C My sister wants to see our museum!

Reading and Comprehension

Fact file: light

Light:

- comes from the sun and the stars
- travels many thousands of kilometres in a split second
- travels faster than sound
- is slowed down a tiny bit by some things such as glass and water
- can cause sunburn. When you wear sunscreen you stop harmful light rays burning through your skin.

1 What does light come from?

A people

B animals

C the sun

2 What can light travel faster than?

A the earth

B the moon

C sound

3 What slows light down a tiny bit?

A shadows

B glass and water

C the sun

4 What can light cause?

A sunburn

B sunscreen

C sun

5 How does light travel?

A very quickly

B very slowly

C It stays still.

6 Which would come first?

A thunder

B lightning

C neither—they'd come at the same time

Spelling

1 Unscramble the letters to make words.

A tghil ______

B thdneru ______

C ousnd ______

2 Which word is spelt correctly?

A earth

B urth

C erth

3 Find two words next to each other in the text that begin with the same sound.

______

Vocabulary

4 Which word from the text means **moves**?

______

5 Circle the word that has a similar meaning to **stop**.

end start begin

6 Cross out the word that does **not** belong.

fast quick slow

7 Add a word from the text to complete the sentence.

I put ______ on my body to stop sunburn.

Grammar

8 Draw lines from the nouns to label the picture:

skin

sunscreen

water

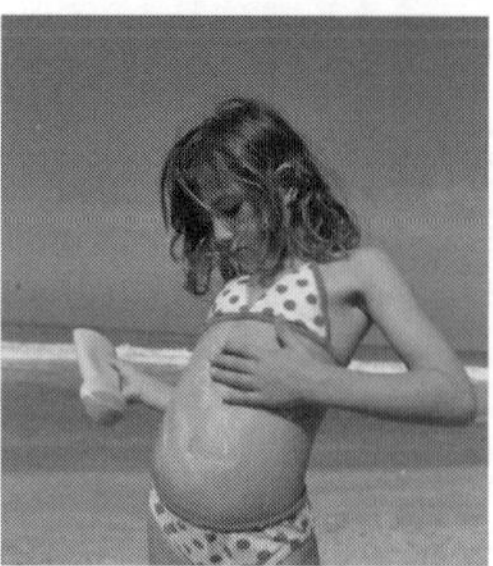

9 Choose a verb from the box to complete the sentence.

started stops makes

Sunscreen ______ sunlight burning your skin.

10 Write an adverb from the text to tell **how**.

Light travels ______.

Punctuation

11 Which sentence is punctuated correctly?

A Did you remember to put on sunscreen?

B Did you remember to put on sunscreen.

C Did you remember to put on sunscreen!

12 Which sentence is punctuated correctly?

A Light moves more quickly than sound?

B light moves more quickly than sound!

C Light moves more quickly than sound.

Reading and Comprehension

The lost princess

Prince Patrick folded his arms. He felt worried. One minute Princess Pearl was in the palace. The next she was gone. He asked the birds if they'd seen her. 'Sorry,' they tweeted sadly. He asked the frogs in the pond. 'No,' they sobbed. He'd already looked in the forest. Where could she be?

1. What did Prince Patrick do with his arms?
   - **A** waved them about
   - **B** shook them
   - **C** folded them

2. How did Prince Patrick feel?
   - **A** sad and worried
   - **B** sad
   - **C** worried

3. What did the birds reply?
   - **A** tweet
   - **B** sorry
   - **C** no

4. What did the frogs say?
   - **A** no
   - **B** yes
   - **C** maybe

5. Where had Prince Patrick last seen Princess Pearl?
   - **A** in the forest
   - **B** in the palace
   - **C** by the pond

6. Why are the birds sad?
   - **A** They know where to find Princess Pearl.
   - **B** Birds are always sad.
   - **C** They can't help Prince Patrick find Princess Pearl.

Spelling

1 Unscramble the letters to make words.

A grofs ______________

B rpncei ______________

C dribs ______________

2 Which word is spelt correctly?

A asked

B arsked

C asced

3 Find two words next to each other in the text that begin with the same sound.

____

Vocabulary

4 Which word from the text means **upset**?

____

5 Circle the word that has a similar meaning to **next**.

then before soon

6 Cross out the word that does **not** belong.

already after now

7 Add a word from the text to complete the sentence.

The prince could not find his

______________.

Grammar

8 Draw lines from the nouns to label the picture:

prince

arms

bird

9 Choose a verb from the box to complete the sentence.

saw	looked	watch

Have you ______________ in the forest yet?

10 Write an adverb from the text to tell **how**.

How did the birds tweet?

____

Punctuation

11 Which sentence is punctuated correctly?

A have you looked for the princess?

B Have you looked for the princess!

C Have you looked for the princess?

12 Which sentence is punctuated correctly?

A The princess is lost!

B The princess is lost?

C The princess is lost.

Reading and Comprehension

1 Choose a word from the box to go in the spaces.

shoes	books	sun	here	school	badly	play

Dear Uncle Ugg

I have started ______________________ in Australia now. We keep our ______________________ on in the classroom! I have a backpack for my ______________________. I wear a hat to keep off the ______________________ when we ______________________ outside or go on visits. I miss Japan ______________________ but I like it ______________________ too.

Love
Akiko

2 Choose a word from the box to go in the spaces.

pouches	now	knit	baby	mothers	warm	wool

Right ______________________ the Wildlife Workers are helping ______________________ possums. We rescue them when their ______________________ die or are hurt. Sadly, there are many of them. We must keep them ______________________ when they are out of their mothers' ______________________. Can you help us ______________________ pouches for them? You will need needles and ______________________.

The Wildlife Workers

Spelling

3 Add nouns to label the picture.

____

____

____

Vocabulary

4 Circle the word that means **worried**.

upset happy calm

5 Circle the word that has a similar meaning to **hurt**.

heard harmed helped

6 Circle the word that means **not moving**.

still wriggling waving

7 Cross out the word that does **not** belong.

light dark sunless

Grammar

8 Choose a verb from the box to complete each sentence.

quickly	badly	Sadly

A I hurt my toenail ______________________.

B She could run very ______________________.

C ______________________, the possum was hurt.

Punctuation

9 Write this sentence correctly.

do animals leave tracks in the bush

____

Reading

My favourite things

The things I like to do best are:

- ride my big bike
- catch the light rail around the city
- write stories
- visit the country and watch for animals
- dig in the garden with my spade
- play in the sand with my bucket when we visit the beach
- save pictures of cars and planes.

by Noah

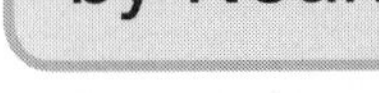

1. What does Noah like to ride?

   A his car

   B his plane

   C his bike

2. Where are the animals Noah likes to see?

   A in the country

   B in the zoo

   C in the city

3. What does Noah use to dig with in the garden?

   A his bucket

   B his spade

   C his bike

4. What does Noah like to play with in the sand?

   A his spade

   B his bucket

   C his cars

5. Where does Noah live?

   A in the country

   B in the city

   C at the beach

6. Where does Noah mainly like to spend his time?

   A indoors

   B at the beach

   C outdoors

NAPLAN-STYLE 4 CONVENTIONS OF LANGUAGE TEST

Spelling

1 Which word is spelt correctly

A annimals **B** animals **C** animmals

2 Find the spelling mistake and write the word correctly on the line.

What do you lyke doing? ______________________

3 Which two words next to each other in the text begin with the same sounds?

____

Vocabulary

4 Which word is similar in meaning to **best**?

most first least

5 Which word means the same as the underlined words?

I like looking at animals in the bush.

A watching **B** following **C** hearing

Grammar

6 Which verb completes the sentence correctly?

I ____________ a sandcastle at the beach yesterday.

A builded **B** built **C** build

7 Circle the words that tell **where** in this sentence.

We drove around the city in our new car.

Punctuation

8 Which sentence is punctuated correctly?

A I like to collect pictures?

B I like to collect pictures!

C I like to collect pictures.

Reprinted 2019, 2020 (twice), 2022

Updated in 2023 for the NSW Curriculum and Australian Curriculum Version 9.0 changes

Reprinted 2024

ISBN 978 1 74125 609 3

Pascal Press
PO Box 250
Glebe NSW 2037
(02) 9198 1748
www.pascalpress.com.au

Publisher: Vivienne Joannou
Project editor: Rosemary Peers and Mark Dixon
Edited by Rosemary Peers and Mark Dixon
Answers checked by Glenda Walsh
Cover and page design by Kim Webber
Typeset by Julianne Billington (lj Design)
Printed by Vivar Printing/Green Giant Press